IN THE MOUNTAINS OF MORAZAN

ortrait of a Returned Refugee Community in El Salvador

Mandy Macdonald & Mike Gatehouse

The Latin America Bureau is an independent research and publishing organisation.
It works to broaden public understanding of human rights and social and economic justice in Latin America and the Caribbean.

First published in the UK in 1995 by the Latin America Bureau (Research and Action) Ltd, 1 Amwell Street, London EC1R 1UL

© Mandy Macdonald and Mike Gatehouse

ISBN 0 906156 94 7

Editor: Helen Collinson

Cover photograph: Jenny Matthews
Cover design: Andy Dark
Photographs: Jenny Matthews and Jenny Matthews/Network, El Salvador Committee for Human Rights (ESCHR), Mike George and Mike Gatehouse
Maps: Department of Geography, University College London

Printed and bound by Russell Press, Nottingham NG7 3HN
Trade distribution in UK by Central Books, 99 Wallis Road, London E9 5LN
Distribution in North America by Monthly Review Press, 122 West 27th Street, New York, NY 10001

Contents

El Salvador

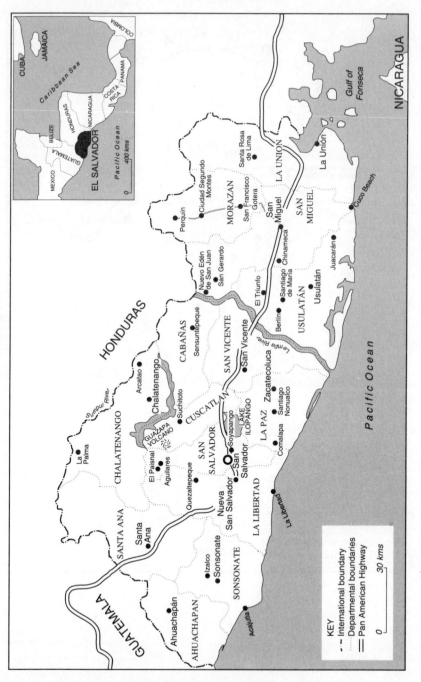

KEY
- – · – International boundary
- ·········· Departmental boundaries
- ═══ Pan American Highway

Morazán

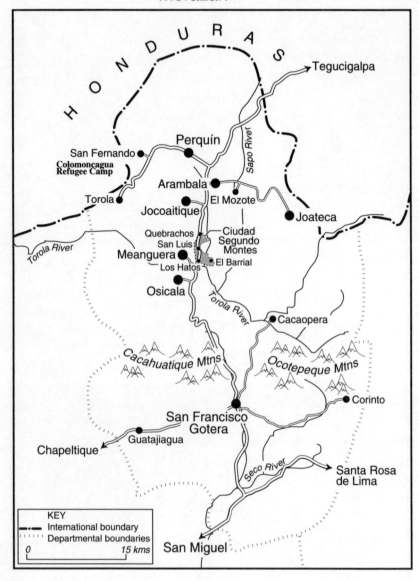

KEY
- ∙—∙ International boundary
- ⋯⋯ Departmental boundaries

0   15 kms

Ciudad Segundo Montes
Morazán

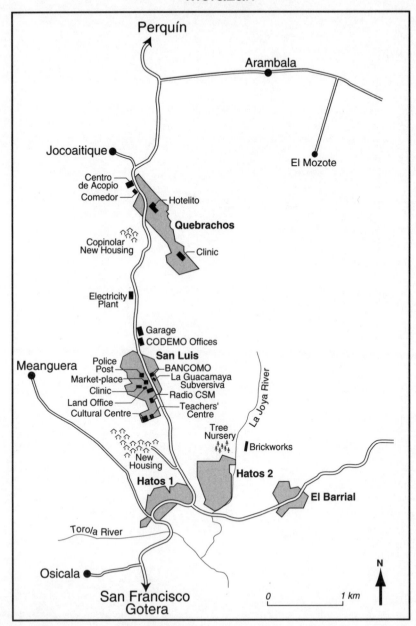

Perquín

Arambala

El Mozote

Jocoaitique

Centro de Acopio

Comedor

Hotelito

Quebrachos

Copinolar New Housing

Clinic

Electricity Plant

Garage

CODEMO Offices

San Luis

Police Post

Market-place

Clinic

Land Office

Cultural Centre

BANCOMO

La Guacamaya Subversiva

Radio CSM

Teachers' Centre

Meanguera

La Joya River

Tree Nursery

Brickworks

New Housing

Hatos 1

Hatos 2

El Barrial

Toro/a River

Osicala

San Francisco Gotera

N

0   1 km

Preface

In November 1989, in the midst of the most intense fighting seen in ten years of civil war, a large group of refugees returned on foot to El Salvador, Central America. They came from Colomoncagua, just across the border in Honduras, where they had been living for the past nine years. They were determined to return home, war or no war. Over the next four months all 8,000 refugees in the camp returned to their homeland in a carefully planned and highly organised repatriation, bringing with them every piece of equipment, plank of wood, corrugated iron – even the nails used in building the refugee housing.

They pitched camp on empty hillsides near Meanguera, in northern Morazán, at the centre of the area from which most of their families had fled. The land was almost entirely deserted, deliberately devastated and emptied of civilian population in 1980-81 by the Salvadorean army, which was intent on destroying the guerrillas of the FMLN. The US-trained forces had used a tactic known as 'draining the sea', to deny the guerrillas (the 'fish') support by the simple expedient of eliminating the civilian population in one of their most important strongholds.

The returnees called their new settlement Ciudad Segundo Montes, after a distinguished Jesuit priest, Fr Segundo Montes, who had befriended them in Colomoncagua. Fr Montes was head of the sociology department and director of the Human Rights Institute at the UCA, the Universidad Centroamericana José Simeón Cañas in San Salvador. During the 1980s he had conducted a series of studies of refugees and population displaced internally by the war in El Salvador. Deeply impressed by what he saw, he regarded the refugees and the society they had created in the camps as offering a real alternative to the poor. "I thought there was no future for El Salvador," he told them, "but when I saw your model of organisation and development, I changed my mind."

Fr Montes did not live to see how this model would develop when the refugees repatriated. On 16 November 1989, during the hours of curfew, he and five other Jesuit priests, together with their housekeeper and her daughter, were dragged from their house at the university and assassinated by members of the Salvadorean armed forces. They had been targeted precisely because they were the country's most articulate campaigners for peace and justice.

Perhaps the best memorial to the Jesuit martyrs, to the murdered Archbishop, Oscar Arnulfo Romero, and to the thousands of other civilians killed in the Salvadorean civil war, were the Peace Accords signed in Mexico City, under the auspices of the United Nations, on 16 January 1992. In no small part, the Accords were possible because of the determination of the Salvadorean people to have peace. One of the most impressive testimonials to that desire was the return and resettlement of refugees and displaced people.

Today, despite delays and compromises, the Peace Accords are still holding, and elections have been held. El Salvador is no longer a country at war, yet the extremes of poverty which fuelled the war remain, and government and the presidency remain firmly in the hands of the far right. The spotlight of attention has turned from the demobilisation of guerrilla and government armies to the question of how the poor and the marginalised can fight in peacetime to create a new and more equitable society. For anyone studying this question, the new community of Ciudad Segundo Montes, not yet five years old, is a good place to begin.

*****

The world, or at least that portion of it in which 'Western' values predominate, is passing through a curious moment in history, characterised by a profound mistrust of and hostility towards collective organisation and action of all kinds. Not only socialism, but most forms of state and collective ownership, cooperatives, trade unions, community groups, public services, even municipal and local government are perceived as being inefficient, obstacles to the functioning of the market, and inimical to individual interests.

In such a climate, any attempt to preserve or extend collective values and structures confronts enormous difficulties on the economic, social and ideological fronts. For the people of Ciudad Segundo Montes, peace, in the military sense, has arrived, but the real war is just beginning. Although they inhabit an isolated and neglected rural area in a distant, tiny, and impoverished country, the nature of their struggle will be instantly recognisable to people in Europe, the USA and many parts of Latin America, Africa and Asia. Their community, its achievements and the difficulties it confronts, provide us with a microcosm from which to learn lessons of almost universal application.

*****

We had visited the Colomoncagua refugee camp several times during the 1980s while we were working in London for the El Salvador Committee for Human Rights and other related agencies. As soon as we heard of the repatriation, we formed the idea of visiting the new community and attempting to describe its progress. It took us two years to find funding for the research and writing and two more years to complete the writing. We have been helped by research grants from Action Aid, Quaker Peace & Service and Save the Children Fund (UK), Catholic Relief Services (USA), NOVIB (Holland), and the Project Counselling Service for Refugees (Costa Rica).

The delay brought some benefits. Many of the most difficult challenges and dramatic changes at Ciudad Segundo Montes have come about as a result of the Peace Accords, and we could not have begun to chronicle these if we had started earlier. In the meantime, others have produced excellent accounts of the Colomoncagua period and the repatriation itself, notably Steve and Beth Cagan in their beautiful book, *This Promised Land, El Salvador* (Rutgers University Press, 1991).

The two of us, and Jenny Matthews, who took many of the photographs in this book, visited Ciudad Segundo Montes separately in November 1990, January 1991, and July, August-September and November 1992. We collected nearly sixty hours of taped interviews, scores of documents and hundreds of photographs. In piecing together a narrative, we have told the story as though it were of a single visit, weaving together real events, fragments of interviews and conversations in a reconstructed but not fictional scenario. However, in doing so we have sought at all times to be faithful to our sources, and to the truth as we perceived it and as the people of the Community attempted to convey it to us. In the same spirit, we have kept to a minimum our own political analysis and tried to let the different actors speak for themselves.

El Salvador has only just emerged from a protracted civil war of exceptional violence and bitterness. We expected members of the Community to be very reserved and to tell us little. The reverse was true, and we were amazed at the openness with which almost everyone spoke to us about their own experiences and part in the conflict. Most of the names in the narrative are those that were used by the people we interviewed. However, the peace itself is fragile, and there are few guarantees against reprisal, so a few names we changed or omitted. We have also respected the anonymity of some of the foreign aid workers and volunteers who spoke to us, because their more critical judgments could jeopardise their working relations with the Community.

*****

Scores of people have helped us in our task, and have been patient and generous with their support. We would like to thank in particular: Francisco Alvarez, Catherine Bell, Marigold Best, Leigh Binford, Steve and Beth Cagan, Graham Denyer, Clare Dixon, Duncan Green, Sr Pamela Hussey, Gordon Hutchison, Sue Keen, Kath Lynch, Ana Eugenia Marín, Pauline Martin, Kate Roberts, Phyllis Robinson, Sara Shannon, the Sisters of St Clare in San Francisco Gotera, and Voices on the Border; the many aid agency workers and international volunteers; but above all to the people of Ciudad Segundo Montes, who tolerated, trusted and inspired us.

Mandy Macdonald
Mike Gatehouse

July 1994

1
The Bridge

The bridge, arrived at suddenly on a road winding slowly northward and upward, crosses the river Torola, which slices the northern part of the province of Morazán neatly off from the rest like the top off a boiled egg. A narrow, lightly constructed bailey bridge thrown across the Torola's shallow, rapid waters, it is unexpectedly new and shiny. Its silvery girders positively sparkle in the sun. The roadway is made of baulks of timber that jump and clack as vehicles cross.

The bridge is here because Ciudad Segundo Montes is here. The refugees' return was the beginning of the end of the region's isolation, an announcement that northern Morazán was no longer just a war zone, but a place where people lived. With the war still raging, the people of Ciudad Segundo Montes negotiated with the Salvadorean government and the national liberation guerrilla forces, the FMLN (*Frente Farabundo Martí para la Liberación National*), for the construction of a bridge across the Torola explicitly for civilian use. On 20 June 1990, the new bridge, built with funds donated by the United Nations High Commission for Refugees (UNHCR), was completed and vehicles could cross the river on the only paved road in northern Morazán for the first time in seven years.

The original bridge had been blown up in 1983 by FMLN guerrillas attempting to foil a major army push into Morazán, which by then was regarded as a 'controlled zone', a semi-liberated area under the effective control of the rebels. The agreement on strictly non-military use of the new bridge was violated several times by both sides before the final peace agreement was signed on 16 January 1992; but the bridge has come to symbolise the reuniting of northern Morazán with the rest of El Salvador. It is also a monument to the determination and political audacity of the people of Ciudad Segundo Montes.

As refugees, these people were renowned for being extraordinarily organised, politically united, and creative in the way they coped with exile. Imprisoned in a permanently militarised refugee camp at Colomoncagua, for years they resisted all attempts to force them to return to El Salvador or to go somewhere else in Honduras against their will. When they finally came home, the same determination, the same communal organisation, was in evidence. The years in exile had given them a new vision, too: they had learned that they were stronger collectively than individually, and they wanted to build a new kind of community on that strength, something that had never been attempted before in rural El Salvador.

In England, we followed their story and supported their struggles. British people sent money and supplies for their craft and semi-industrial workshops in Colomoncagua and have continued to support development projects in Ciudad Segundo Montes. Now, in August 1992, we have come to take up the story of this extraordinary social and political experiment, Segundo Montes City.

*****

War slashed Morazán in two. Always one of the poorest and most inaccessible regions of El Salvador, in the late 1970s it became the base for the ERP (*Ejército Revolucionario Popular*), one of the five guerrilla organisations that made up the FMLN. Northern Morazán became a major theatre of war, progressively depopulated in the course of the early 1980s as the armed forces carried out first a series of vast ground sweeps through the mountain villages in 1980 and 1981, then intense aerial bombing campaigns in 1983-4. The FMLN proved harder to dislodge than the civilians, however, and by 1983 the army had retreated from all military positions north of the Torola. After the bridge on the Perquín road was blown up, the north of the province was isolated not only militarily but also from any government services, sealing the 'conflictive' north off from the 'pacified' south. Nearly all of the area fom the Honduran border down to the river, and stretching east to Corinto, became an 'FMLN-controlled zone', referred to locally as simply 'the Zone'.

South of the river, it was the government forces, based in their large barracks in the departmental capital, San Francisco Gotera, who called the shots. The civilian population either supported them or were terrorised into keeping quiet. Unless they were rich enough to pay handsome bribes, their sons were forcibly conscripted into the army and involved in action against the FMLN guerrillas and any civilians considered remotely sympathetic to them. Trade and transport may have brought northern and southern Morazán back into contact, but distrust between them still runs deep, and reconciliation, even after the peace agreements and the ending of the war, will be a long process.

*****

Our jeep coasts down to this new Torola bridge and crosses with some caution and much clanking. On the other side, we lurch almost immediately into a bomb-crater in the unrepaired road: the first of many. The landscape changes almost at once, too. Some of this is natural: north of the river, the ground is steeper, more broken, steadily rising towards Perquín, 1,200 metres above sea level, and the Honduran border beyond, higher and grander still. But the change is largely the result of war. Bombed, mined, burned, and abandoned, this land has been virtually uncultivated for a decade. The green fields of southern Morazán give way here to wild, scrub-covered hillsides, sparsely shaded by the trees that got away, and raw red scars of bare earth, punctuated with tiny cornfields and, here and there, newly reforested areas.

South of the Torola, the hills are striped with fields of dark grey-green maguey (*agave americana*), marching across the slopes in regimented rows. The swordlike, fibrous leaves of the maguey are the source of sisal, which was the traditional cottage industry of Morazán before the war. But here, north of the river, the maguey stops:

"From the river northwards," people tell us, "all those crops were completely destroyed by the war. You see, the soldiers wanted to see everything done away with, down to the vegetation. They set fire to it every six months: trees, plants, fruit trees, houses, everything."

A kilometre beyond the bridge, the road to Meanguera village forks off to the left. The village, a mile or so from the turnoff, is the centre of the municipality of Meanguera, within which CSM, Ciudad Segundo Montes, is situated. Although it never went over wholly to the FMLN in the war, it was badly damaged and many of its people fled. Its relations with CSM are ambiguous, and its position as a municipal centre has become anomalous with the creation of CSM, a community several times its size, within its jurisdiction. From here on, houses appear again. Not the traditional russet-tiled, deep-eaved adobe houses nestling close to the ground, or the newer breeze-block and cement boxes painted in faded pastels, that are common south of the river. These dwellings are made of wooden planks and fibre-board, roofed with galvanised iron. There is lots of plastic sheeting and cardboard. They are dusty and earth-coloured and ramshackle. None of them is yet three years old, and they manage to look raw and temporary and at the same time as if they've been here forever. Many of the houses near the road are also little shops: crates of empty Coke and pop bottles are piled outside, placards advertise cigarettes, aspirin, soap. There are more and more people on the road: a constant and purposeful toing-and-froing. Children are everywhere: self-importantly

Torola river. The new bridge has opened up
northern Morazán after years of isolation.

Jenny Matthews/Network

carrying books and bright-coloured rucksacks, scurrying along on some errand, larking about with a homemade football made of newspaper bound with string. The landscape south of the Torola bridge, while not deserted, is certainly not bustling: a quiet, cowed countryside, keeping its head down. On the north bank, radiating a kind of raw, frontier-town energy, Ciudad Segundo Montes both looks and feels different.

In fact the Community announces itself explicitly – or rather, is announced. Beside the road, a large blue and white hoarding proclaims magniloquently: 'Ciudad Segundo Montes Community: Financed by the European Community'. What, all of it? As we get to know the place better, we will find this boast qualified by other hoardings, labels and plaques: together with a host of foreign development agencies, the EC is contributing to this health programme, that school, these new houses, a whole range of productive projects. For one of the things that notably makes CSM 'different' is the extent to which it has attracted, and has relied upon, foreign aid. In Colomoncagua, the refugees survived entirely on aid and used it well. When they returned, the political importance of the repatriation in the context of the peace process, and the innovativeness of the people's plan to found a new town, made the repatriated community a key project for many aid donors. Aid has been a catalyst, a cushion, and a trap.

*****

San Luis is the geographical and administrative centre of Ciudad Segundo Montes. The main road runs straight through it. On one side of the road is a row of small shops in a long barrack-like building, some run by the Community, some private; on the other a small marketplace full of colour and life. Now that it's easy to cross the Torola, small traders drive up from the town of San Francisco Gotera every day and rent stalls from CSM. Rough wooden trestle tables and iron clothes racks behind them are bright with T-shirts, cotton frocks, jeans and skimpily-cut polyester shirts, shoes, cheap cosmetics and plastic hair ornaments and combs. Cheerful and streetwise, the stallholders call out to each other and to people going by. Under the eaves of the shops opposite, people keep out of the sun while they wait for buses or lifts – practically every vehicle will stop at San Luis.

Behind the market stalls and enclosing them in a rough crescent are three buildings that survived the war relatively intact and have been restored as community buildings, a reminder that there was a village here before the war. On the left, the Communal Bank of Morazán, BANC-

OMO, the only two-storey building in CSM, painted pastel blue and white and with its name and logo in white on a red banner hanging from the upper veranda. That uniformed man sitting nonchalantly on the porch step is Martín, a member of the Community's small police force. Next to the bank is a low, white building, half rebuilt; three or four men are hammering away at its new roof-timbers, while two women in straw hats and matching apricot frocks are mixing concrete for its floor. This building is to be a supermarket; the shop sign is up already at the roadside: 'SuperMontes Stores. With the lowest prices.'

The third of this little group of buildings is the *comedor*, or café, of San Luis, called La Guacamaya Subversiva. This is a pun understandable only to locals: the café is named after a nearby hamlet, La Guacamaya, wiped out by the military, like so many others, for its presumed support of the 'subversives', as the government always called the FMLN. And La Guacamaya Subversiva was also the name of a famous and hugely popular satirical radio programme broadcast during the war by Radio Venceremos, the guerrilla radio station. But guacamaya also means parrot, strictly speaking the large and brilliant macaw – which features on a T-shirt screen-printed and sold by CSM's External Relations department.

The atmosphere of the Guacamaya is, well, Country and Western. Its wooden signboard is brown and rustic. Dusty bunting hangs from the ceiling, possibly left over from last Christmas or some other big day. Plump Tina cultivates a saloonkeeper image, with dangly ear-rings, a red blouse made of something shiny, and a cigarette. San Luis being the only one of CSM's five settlements to have electricity, the café has a big refrigerator full of cold soft drinks and beer, and a cassette deck which is always belting out music. Most of the time the music is from a twenty-year-old recording of protest songs by a Venezuelan left-wing band, Los Guaraguao, called Casas de Cartón (Cardboard Houses). Coffee, hot and weak and surprisingly refreshing in the heat of the day, comes in plastic beakers and is drunk at the new concrete picnic tables and benches that have just been installed in a yard outside the café. Emaciated dogs, all spiky ribs and begging eyes, hang around hoping for scraps. Little boys are also crawling around our feet, absorbed in games of marbles: the tiled floor of the café and the flat, swept ground outside it provide the perfect terrain.

The scene is one of small-town bustle. But there will be constant reminders that this village is a phoenix rising out of ruin and death. We talk a little with two elderly men at the next table. One of them tells us this story. In front of the bank stands a large, old tree, its branches spreading like a benediction over the bank building and the little stalls. But it was from those branches, in the early 1980s, that government soldiers on the rampage through Morazán hanged local women and children. This is a place where ghosts flutter from the trees and the bones of the dead crunch underfoot. Terror and desolation have left it so recently that their presence hangs on the air like perfume a moment after its wearer leaves the room.

*****

We cross the tarmac road and turn up a track opposite the marketplace, dusty and unshaded in the unforgiving midday glare. The assorted buildings on either side are public offices, the Community's administrative centre. On the right, the town planning department, Urban Development (*Desarrollo Urbano*) and the Land Office (*Oficina de Tierras*), recently opened to record who owns what land within the area the Community occupies. Behind them, the San Luis school, day-nursery and clinic, housed in long sheds of weathered wooden planks, greyish-brown or whitewashed. The neat white adobe-style cottage on the left-hand side is the 'Show House', built as an experiment when the design and building materials for the Community's permanent housing were being decided. No one lives in it: it is earmarked as the office for the national telephone company, ANTEL. Engineers have installed the lines, but the exchange connection has yet to materialise. To make a phone call from CSM, you have to go south of the Torola, to Osicala, about an hour's journey.

Nearby we can hear music – not the canned music from the Guacamaya, but live guitars and a drum kit and the rather plaintive singing style of Salvadorean folk music. It comes from a small house where the Community's music group, the Conjunto Morazán is based.

Another adobe house, a little further on, is divided in two like a semi-detached cottage. One side is occupied by the education department offices, the other by Radio Segundo Montes, which broadcasts for three hours in the morning and three in the evening each day. The radio station and the Conjunto Morazán, together with a photography and video workshop (the small white prefab, unique to CSM in having an air-conditioner) and a press division whose office is down near the marketplace, make up the Department of Social Communication.

When you arrive at Ciudad Segundo Montes, you usually check in with *Relaciones*, the Community's Department of External Relations. In the mid-1980s in Colomoncagua, the refugee community set up a 'Reception Committee' to coordinate the visits of the increasing number of foreign visitors from aid agencies and solidarity organisations. The refugees were famous for the public welcomes they would prepare for visitors: thousands of people would turn out, huge cloth banners with a message of greeting would be hung across the entrance to the refugee camp, there would be music and speeches, and the hapless new arrival, exhausted from a ten-hour drive across Honduras on dirt roads and at least one temper-fraying encounter with the Honduran military, would be expected to make an impromptu speech at whatever level of Spanish he or she could manage.

In CSM, this custom has faded away for the most part: registering with *Relaciones* is now a practical matter, allowing the Community's leaders to know who you are and enabling the visitor to locate a bed for the night. We are welcomed by two friendly women, Rosa and Luisa. Visitors usually stay in guest rooms at the Cultural Centre in San Luis. We choose instead to stay in Quebrachos, the most northerly of the Community's five settlements, closer to the ordinary life of the people, and, at some five hundred feet above San Luis, cooler at night. The rent is ¢5 per night (about 35p!). Luisa, who lives in Quebrachos, will show us our accommodation later. Meanwhile, Rosa takes us to lunch at the Community's cafeteria, and afterwards she will take us on a tour of the workshops.

*****

A shiny white Toyota jeep with the insignia of ONUSAL, the United Nations peace-keeping force, stands on a neatly gravelled parking area on the hill-top. Behind it is the Cultural Centre – a covered area for the Community's meetings and assemblies, and the Community's central eating place, frequented by international workers, visitors, some of the Community leaders, and increasingly by tourists.

Lunch consists of tortilla, the unleavened, pancake-shaped maize bread which is the main constituent of every Salvadorean meal, and *frijoles*, a thick purple paste of pulped kidney beans. We decline the fried plantain, heavy, fibrous and extremely oily. To drink there is Pepsi-Cola, reasonably cold from the fridge.

In a swirl of dust, a second jeep skids to a halt besidethe Community cafeteria. Out jump two figures in smart olive-green uniforms, revolvers at their belts. The older of the two, an athletic figure in his forties with silver-grey hair, looks like a major in the French paratroops. He saunters over to the table where two ONUSAL officers are sitting, greets them affectionately and launches into animated conversation. The other, his driver, lounges against the jeep, one hand on a sub-machine gun slung around his neck, alert and on guard. The army? Here in the Community? "No," explains Rosa, "they are *compas* from the assembly point up by Perquín."

Compas, *compañeros*, comrades, means members of the FMLN, usually guerrilla fighters. In this area of Morazán most are from the ERP, probably the largest of the five separate military-political groupings making up the FMLN. Under the terms of the Peace Accords, the FMLN agreed to concentrate its guerrilla troops in designated assembly points, while they wait to be demobilised and re-integrated into civilian life. The nearest such assembly point is about eight miles north of Ciudad Segundo Montes, by the road into Perquín. We are well aware that north of the Torola river is FMLN territory, but it is somehow a shock to see guerrilla fighters in full uniform, armed, and so evidently at ease.

*****

It's easy to see why visitors come to this spot. It must have one of the finest views in El Salvador. The roughly circular plateau can be scarcely more than 100 yards across. On three sides the ground drops away precipitously four or five hundred feet to a wide plain, extending to the Torola river, about two miles away as the *zopilote* – the ubiquitous vulture of Central America – flies. Beyond the river to the east, the land climbs steeply again, patched with the darker greens of mature woodland and coffee plantations, yielding to conifers higher up, into a single massif crowned by the 7,000 foot volcanic peak of Cacahuatique.

In the valley below near the river is a clump of larger trees on a small bluff, with tile roofs showing through and the hint of a church tower. This is Meanguera, the village within whose boundaries Ciudad Segundo Montes has been built. Meanguera is a *municipio*, a local seat of government with a mayor (a woman called Paz Membreño, a member of the Christian Democrat party, at present living in San Francisco Gotera, and altogether too frightened to return to her town hall).

Close up below the Cultural Centre, bright new orange-red roofs show among the trees amid the clutter of a building site. This must be the big European Community-funded project for new housing, whose sign we saw further down the road.

Northwards the Torola valley curves away, hidden by the land rising steadily upwards towards Jocoaitique and Perquín. The slopes here are densely chequered with *milpa*, the little maize and bean plots sown by every family in Ciudad Segundo Montes. It is the rainy season, and the backdrop of mountains is invested with towers of cloud that mount steadily through the day, balancing precariously on the peaks before tumbling suddenly downwards in the late afternoon, to overwhelm the valleys and the lesser hills of the Community with premature darkness and torrential rain. Southwards the view is softer, a coil of the Torola river glinting in the sun, and the road visible beyond it, zigzagging towards San Francisco Gotera.

*****

Behind us are the huts of the External Relations office and the visitors' guest house. Further on, tin roofs glint among the trees, various jeeps and vehicles are parked, and electricity cables criss-cross the track which leads back down to the tarmac road and the marketplace.

Segundo Montes City? Certainly the initial impression of an urban community is very striking. A good-sized rural village anywhere in Central America is likely to have at most a church, a mayor's office, a post and telecom office, and a school and a clinic (if it is lucky). By comparison, the civic and administrative infrastructure of Ciudad Segundo Montes is enormous. It is one of the most visible signs of its aspirations, or at least the aspirations of its leaders, to establish, in this remote and impoverished rural zone, a centre that is explicitly urban, literate, and distinct from the *campesino* society into which it is inserted. The nature and extent of that insertion is the measure of the success of the Ciudad Segundo Montes experiment.

2
The Workshops

A small group has gathered at the Cultural Centre meeting place, including Juan José, best-known of the leaders of the Community. Three men and two women are sitting on folding metal chairs in a rough semi-circle without a table, talking quietly, an almost apologetic presence in such a large space, silhouetted against the mountains and the clouds. They look worried: they are talking about the difficulties of the recent Community assembly, held on 4 July to discuss Target 2000, the plan put forward by the leadership to transform the Community into a loose association of decentralised, self-sufficient units and activities. Target 2000 is now supposed to be discussed in detail by the workers in each of the Community's ten work areas – Administration and Planning, Production, Distribution, Urban Development, Health, Education, Communication, External Relations, Communal Services, and the Bank.

The roll-call of work areas says much about the nature of this Community – highly organised and centrally planned, its tight structure having evolved during the years in the enclosed refugee camp at Colomoncagua. The repatriation to Morazán took place in the midst of some of the most ferocious fighting of the war, and for the next 18 months the new Community was a civilian enclave in a war zone, quarantined from the rest of the country by a hostile and suspicious army. The same discipline which built the refugee camp also organised the repatriation and created in an abandoned wilderness the infrastructure of an entire town. But now the new bridge across the river, the signing of the Peace Accords and the removal of the army checkpoints have transformed the situation. The Community must change and adapt. It is no longer an island.

The meeting is subdued, for there are serious problems, and it is clear that discussion of the new plan will need to proceed much more slowly than had been hoped. People in the Community are confused and sometimes angry at the scale of change being thrust upon them. They are afraid of losing the standards of living and social services which as refugees they fought so hard to obtain and protect, and which now, paradoxically, are threatened more by the peace process than they were in wartime.

Since distribution of free food (financed by foreign aid) stopped about nine months ago, some families are hungry. Even the minority who have jobs and are paid a small wage by the Community are being told that their area of work must earn an income and become self-sufficient, or face closure. For the rest, the overwhelming problems are no work, not enough land and not enough able-bodied people to farm it even if the land were sufficient.

The present, highly centralised structure of the Community is a major problem. As Juan José says:

"The Community has now become so complex that it can no longer cope with managing all those things which are centralised at present. In the past, it was the war that forced us to centralise everything. Peace has imposed a harsher reality.

The single, integrated structure which the Community had before, worked and is still working almost like a government, as a political organisation, a social organisation, an organisation for production. But it cannot go on like that, because the conditions that produced it have disappeared.

The fact that we have the Peace Accords, that we have the chance for stability, that the FMLN has agreed to participate in the legal structures and constitutional channels, forces us to change too, if we don't want to be out of step."

*****

Rosa comes to collect us for our tour of the workshops. At present, she explains, all of them come under the Community's production organisation, CODEMO. In future, if the suggestions of Target 2,000 are followed, they will become autonomous enterprises, forced to make a profit or close down.

Throughout the 1980s, visitors to the Colomoncagua refugee camp were treated to a tour of the *talleres*, small semi-industrial workshop units which were the camp's showpiece, the visible symbols of the refugees' organisation, industry and progress. By the mid-1980s the tally of workshops included clothing, embroidery, machine-knitting, shoe-making, pottery, musical instrument making, carpentry, furniture, galvanised tinware, metal and welding, radio, and vehicle repair. These supplied a fair proportion of the camp's basic requirements, especially in clothing and footwear, while giving a sense of purpose, employment and training to a significant number of the refugees. They also provided a magnet for aid: the combination of tangible, small-scale projects combining production and training proved almost irresistible to many aid agencies and solidarity groups in Europe, Canada and the US.

When the refugees repatriated in 1989-90, the workshops, like everything else in the camp, were carefully packed up and transported to Ciudad Segundo Montes. As the new Community settled down, the workshops were re-established and resumed production. In the closed environment of the refugee camp, economic viability had never been an issue. The buildings, equipment and raw materials were all provided by the aid agencies, together with technicians to train the refugee workers. The products were distributed free within the camp – the refugees were forbidden by the Honduran authorities to trade, even in the immediate vicinity. And the workers were unpaid volunteers. The workshops functioned in the complete absence of money or even barter.

After the repatriation, many of the workshops simply resumed where they had left off in Colomoncagua. It soon became apparent that some of them were no longer required – knitwear, for instance, was redundant in the much warmer climate of Meanguera. But in the war situation that prevailed, where free movement was prevented by army checkpoints and there was little or no access to external markets, production continued to be geared to supplying the Community's basic needs without any competition.

*****

Children from the San Luis school, their classes over for the afternoon, charge past us as we follow Rosa down to the tarmac road. Despite the heat, most of the boys wear long trousers, and quite a few have peaked baseball caps. The girls are in cotton print dresses or skirt and blouse, long dark hair loose, pinned with a hair-clip or wrapped in a loose bun. Most have a cloth bookbag with a shoulder strap, while one or two have sports-style rucksacks. Each carries a whole cucumber supplied to Community schoolchildren by a grant from a British aid agency. The incongruous sound of crunching cucumber is plainly audible, even amidst the bustle of the roadside market.

A cart lumbers up the hill, drawn by two oxen. Its wheels are rough-hewn, spokeless disks of solid wood with a metal rim. Several of the schoolchildren cadge a lift, while the oxen plod on imperturbably, heads bowed under the heavy wooden yoke.

Three hundred yards uphill from San Luis, a short track leads off to the left to a couple of wooden sheds where piles of metal strips and short pieces of angle-iron are spread across a workbench. A bright point of violet light shows from a welding arc, and there is an acrid smell of burning carbon. This is the Community's metal workshop. The welder is a woman; her assistant, holding and carrying the metal rods, a man. The welding stops and the woman tilts back her mask. Victoria is the supervisor of the workshop.

Nine people work here. Like most of the workshops, metalwork was established in the refugee camp in Colomoncagua. As well as welding and cutting equipment, they have two lathes, one of them large and highly sophisticated, which somehow made the journey across the border. "We make various things," says Victoria. "Doors for the hen houses, for instance; metal crosses for graves; and these school desks." Outside in the sun, two young men, their arms grey to the elbows, are using sponges to daub the metal desk-frames with paint, presumably because they have no brushes or spray equipment.

A storeroom is crammed full of the school desks, metal chair and wooden desktop mounted on an integral metal frame. "We've made 250 of these so far for the schools in the Community. We can make about 60 or 70 per week. Now we have an order for 600 for schools throughout northern Morazán." This seems encouraging: here is a workshop which is producing goods for sale outside the community. "Our main problem", says Victoria, "is lack of storage space. We're constructing a new building, which should help."

Despite a full order book, the atmosphere of the workshop is desultory. Only four out of the complement of nine workers are present. Victoria is obviously deft and skilful as a welder, yet as a supervisor, and spokesperson for a small production unit, she is far from articulate. Her replies to questions are brief, almost monosyllabic. She doesn't appear to have any ambitions for the workshop, or vision of how it might expand, sell more, employ more people. There is a curious reticence, an absence of verve. Somehow, it hadn't been like that in Colomoncagua, when we visited the same workshops there in the 1980s.

Across the road, a large barn-like tin-roofed structure houses the CSM garage. As with so many of the Community's facilities, there is no sign outside, and the passing motorist would have no idea that it was there. Behind it stands a clutter of semi-abandoned vehicles in varying stages of cannibalisation, grass growing up through the open bonnet of an aged Chevrolet pick-up. Under the roof there are four large repair bays, two with an inspection pit dug into the beaten earth floor. There is no sign of a hoist for heavy lifting, and the floor and roof beams of the building would be too weak to support one. A cement block building at one end houses the office and spares department. We are received by the administrator, José Clemente Carrillo, who explains:

"This garage is one of the projects of CODEMO [the Community's production organisation] and we get some financial support from the European Community. We service vehicles and also some of the machinery in the Community. People from the surrounding communities bring their vehicles to us, and we even get a few from south of the river. Then there are the visitors to the Community... I would say it's about half and half, work for the Community, and work on vehicles from outside. This is the only garage in Morazán north of the Torola. So we're well placed for business. Five of us work here and three are trained mechanics. They learnt the trade back in Colomoncagua where we had a repair workshop."

One of the mechanics, Clemente, appears at the doorway, with a length of steel tubing in his hand. "Excuse me, *compañero*. Have we got any tubing this size?" "There must be – try that pile over there." José continues:

"Part of the problem here is the lack of proper tools – we've got very few. The other thing is the spares situation. We don't carry a stock of spares, which makes it difficult to work efficiently. Often we could do the work, if we just had the right parts."

So what happens if someone brings in a vehicle, say, that needs a new clutch?

"At present, we look at the vehicle, tell the owner what parts it needs and he has to get hold of them. Sometimes they have to go to Guatemala to get them.

Do you have any plans to supply spare parts yourselves?

"Not at present, as far as I know. We have an instructor, an Irish mechanic, working with us. Maybe he'll help us solve the spares problem some day."

*****

Behind the garage, another long shed houses the sheetmetal workshop. The coordinator, Juan Alberto Vigil, shows us round. A tall, slightly stooping figure, he has been with this workshop for seven years, supervising its transfer from Colomoncagua to Ciudad Segundo Montes at the time of the repatriations. It was up and running again within six months of arriving in Morazán. There are five paid workers at present and several are quite young, having started work as young boys in Colomoncagua. Juan Alberto, though, is ready to retire, he says; despite his glasses, his sight is failing.

In the storeroom every shelf and bay is stacked with a profusion of objects made of galvanised iron: milk cans, watering cans, buckets, jugs, scoops, measures, water holders of various sizes and shapes, casseroles, troughs, a crude pair of scales, big chicken coops for the poultry farm project, small oil lamps and a curious jug-like container with a long spout which Juan says is a 'smoker for beehives'. At present they are working on *graneros* – cylindrical containers for storing maize. The larger ones are about four feet high and can hold eight sacks of maize – plenty for an average family.

The galvanised sheet is bought in San Miguel. It is cut by hand with shears, shaped and then soldered. The products appear to be well-made and uniform. Some are sold through the shops at San Luis, some directly to callers at the workshop. People are coming from as far away as Perquín and San Francisco Gotera to buy the products, and about half the total production of the workshop is now sold outside the Community.

This workshop seems more dynamic, certainly than the garage. But a few days later, Norbert, one of the international workers gave us a striking illustration of some of the problems, even here. Not long ago he had hitched a lift from a passing pickup truck. In the back was a pile of galvanised iron watering cans. The driver explained that he had just come from San Francisco Gotera, where he had bought 22, the entire stock he could find in the town; he had really wanted 50. Norbert told him about the CSM sheetmetal workshop. The man hadn't known of its existence, although he often passed it on the road, not least because it had no sign and no name.

*****

Next to the metalwork shop, work is going ahead steadily on a new building which will house the Community's technical school. In the refugee camp at Colomoncagua classes were given in mechanical drawing, car repair and furniture design. In CSM, classes have already started in temporary premises in San Luis in typing, agronomy, manual skills such as machine sewing and embroidery, technical drawing and photography.

Sheetmetal workshop   Jenny Matthews/Network

Given the desperate lack of managerial, administrative and commercial experience in the Community, the technical school has a vital role to play, but it may be some time before people with adequate skills and training are available to staff the numerous projects and autonomous enterprises at CSM. Some skilled technicians are being brought in from outside, and increasingly these are Salvadoreans rather than international volunteers. The CSM leaders, however, are afraid of 'opportunists who put on a façade of being this or that kind of *técnico*, but who have their own agenda'.

*****

Just beyond the road are two small sheds in a fenced enclosure where electricity poles converge on a switching sub-station. Around twenty oil drums are stacked outside, and there is the steady hum of heavy machinery. This is the Community's own power station. The diesel-powered generators work from about 8.00am to 8.00pm, supplying 230 volts AC to all the workshops, the administration offices (where it powers lighting, photocopiers and computers), the bank, the radio station and the cafeterias at San Luis. But there the power lines stop. There is no power anywhere except at San Luis.

Before the war, northern Morazán had electricity. About a mile north of Quebrachos, on a hill-top by the roadside close to the Jocoaitique turning, stand the ruins of a large sub-station, pylons crumpled, jagged metal arms tendering broken insulators to an indifferent sky. This and other key installations were blown up early in the war, the wires and cables long since stripped and commandeered by the FMLN or the army, or both. Here and there by the roadside, peasant households use the sheathed copper cables for washing lines. In Perquín, electricity poles line the streets, some still with their lighting globes intact, but the sky is innocent of the essential tracery of wire, and the nights remain stubbornly dark.

It will be a long time before electricity returns to most of the zone. The CSM plant is probably the only mains electricity system north of the Torola. The generators have spare capacity, perhaps enough to provide at least street lighting for the whole Community, but the cost of posts and wiring would be considerable, and at present there are no plans to extend the grid.

The afternoon is now well advanced, as Rosa leads us back down the hill to the Cultural Centre, exhausted from our tour and dehydrated from the heat and dust.

3
Quebrachos

Luisa is waiting to accompany us to Quebrachos, where we will sleep. We collect our bags from the External Relations office and walk back down to the *calle negra*, the 'black road' – the only tarmac road in northern Morazán. At the San Luis marketplace, people are streaming out of workplaces and clustering at the bus stop, waiting for buses or lifts to Quebrachos, Jocoaitique, Perquín. The stallholders have packed up long ago and gone home to Osicala and San Francisco Gotera, south of the Torola.

The road winds slowly up towards Quebrachos and the high mountains. The land is very broken, honeycombed with small, steep-sided valleys, fast filling now with evening shadow. Once, tiny little settlements or isolated farms drowsed in all these little cwms; now, they are endless green scabbed with raw red earth where the land has been cleared for planting. San Luis straggles along the road for a mile or so. As we pass the office of the Community's production department, perched like a sentinel on a little cliff overhanging the road, Luisa recalls how she watched from its windows, one day in 1990, while a long line of government infantry passed in single file, each soldier carefully keeping his twenty yards' distance from the one in front. It took half an hour for them to go by. "It's quite something to be able to travel on this road now without fear," says Luisa.

There are still occasional people in uniform on the road; but these days they are members of the FMLN fighting forces, now renamed the National Democratic Army (END), handsome in their olive green. A teenage girl and boy (the *compas* are almost without exception young) flag us down for a lift and cling onto the tail of the pickup, laughing. They are on their way back to the Pueblo Viejo camp near Perquín.

*****

Five kilometres north of San Luis, Quebrachos is the largest of CSM's five settlements, with a population of 2,456, just over 30 per cent of the total population of CSM. It sprawls out in several directions from its 'entrance', where a dirt road forks off from the *calle negra*. Occupying a broad, open plateau several hundred feet higher than San Luis, it is pleasantly cool and breezy. As we arrive, shadows are lengthening across a grassy football field fringed with wooden buildings and trees. On the far side, a steep drop into a valley and a view of the El Mozote mountain in the distance, and in one corner a little banana grove. A vivid shoal of little girls is surging back and forth across it in some kind of ball game, while a couple of older girls, deep in conversation, take a piglet for a walk on a rope lead along one of the narrow paths criss-crossing the grass.

Before the war, Quebrachos was a thriving little village of a hundred or so houses, well-sited on the main road north to Perquín, with land for subsistence crops and pasture for cattle. There was a 'provisional' school with two teachers, teaching up to fourth grade. Plans for a larger school were dashed by the war. Everything was destroyed. But the new Quebrachos perhaps has some of the old sense of a busy community life, with its small shops, school, clinic, and chapel, and the bus stop where people meet as much to chat as to wait for transport. Quebrachos also has the *hotelito* – the 'little hotel' – where visitors can stay for ¢5 (about 35p) a night. It's a large barrack-like building furnished with a few dozen camp beds and often, after rain, the odd *matacaballos* ('horse-killer'), a venomous spider the size of a tarantula.

A little way along the main road, under the wing of the huge, unfinished Centro de Acopio, the Community's main warehouse and distribution centre, is the Quebrachos cafeteria, set back a little from the road. Unlike the Community's other two eating-places, it is a closed-in, cosy little building, where it is possible to sit for hours talking out an evening storm in dry comfort. A team of three women, Pacita, Helena, and Esperanza, soft-voiced and kindly, cook and serve simple meals. Several of the international workers live in Quebrachos, and this is where they eat. The cafeteria also serves groups staying at the hotel, and, less frequently, drivers passing by on their way up to Perquín and beyond. But all three cafeterias really exist for people who are not of the Community. The citizens of CSM are not in the habit of eating out.

*****

By 7.00pm, when the meal is over, it is quite dark, and beyond the little group at the table, their faces softly illuminated by two candles in pop bottles, the café is in deep shadow. Paul and François, two international workers who live in Quebrachos, are here, and also Jean, who is on an evaluation visit for an aid agency. At one end of the table sits Tomás, a catechist with long experience of pastoral work in both Colomoncagua

Cultural Centre café in San Luis. The Community's
cafés are frequented mainly by foreigners

Mike Gatehouse

and CSM. Nestling next to him, two of his grandchildren follow the talk
like a tennis match, big dark eyes darting from speaker to speaker. Juan
José has looked in to let us know of an important meeting in the next few
days, an Assembly of the Community's teachers.

"The teachers are going to discuss the Community's general objectives
for the next eight years," Juan José tells us. "Following on from the last
General Assembly, we're trying to reach consensus on these objectives
by consulting all the work areas one by one." They'll talk about how the
Community should respond to the challenges of peace – how, for instance,
to prepare for up to a thousand demobilised FMLN combatants who could
soon be coming to settle in CSM; how to speed the Community's
integration into the region; what people think of the new wage policy, the
promotion of private economic initiatives. "The discussion promises to
be heated", says Paul, "because the list of issues to be discussed left out
the one question that worries people most: will the encouragement of
individual money-making projects, and the gradual reduction in aid put
things like free health, education and other social services at risk?

Tomás is concerned that this may happen. "I agree that changes are
necessary; but I don't think that the change from working in community,

collective work, to individual work is very good, because you don't get people supporting each other, and it's harder for everyone to work. I don't much like the idea of our drifting apart, losing the community vision."

"The peace has been an upheaval to everyone", says Juan José, "and we're no exception. It's really forced us to rethink the whole direction we need to take to achieve the Community we want. And it's ironic, but one of the first things we've noticed as a result of the peace is that things are getting tougher. To some extent, I think, the war encouraged us to think that there'd always be aid, that at the end of the day the civilian population wouldn't be left alone and unsupported. But now there's peace, the donors are beginning to impose conditions that they didn't before."

"Realistically," Jean says, "many of the productive activities can't be subsidised in the long term. They have to become self-sufficient if CSM is to become a normal community. That's why aid agencies want to support production projects, things that will help give the Community an economic niche locally – and further afield."

"But CSM isn't a normal community," Paul argues. "It's a community with a very high proportion of old people and small children, and lots of households headed by women – not to mention over 300 war-disabled people. Can a community like this really go for self-sufficient economic production? Won't it always have to be subsidised to some extent?"

Full self-sufficiency has always been a goal of the Community, Juan José insists. "We recognised that the community in exile was utopian. We all worked for the benefit of all, without expecting any more reward than the satisfaction of doing a job in the communal interest. But we always knew that once we returned to El Salvador, we'd have to start coping with money – although we were still determined to go on working communally, for the communal good. At the same time, we could see that a legacy of the refuge, where we were a totally assisted community, was to produce a very dependent mentality in people. They felt helpless if they thought aid was going to be taken away from them.

"So in July 1991 the General Assembly decided to embark on a new economic model. We actively invited people to start up individual enterprises by offering them credit, and we started to introduce money and wages into the communal work areas. When the food aid petered out at the end of 1991, it became urgent for us to start developing commercial relations outside the Community.

"On top of all that, we're facing the social and economic consequences of the Peace Accords – the process of rejoining the rest of the country, legalising the Community, getting the government to carry out its responsibilities. And finally there are the demobilised combatants, and the question of what work they will do. The women have already expressed concern that these men are going to replace women in the workplace."

The problem, it seems to us, is that the Community is now learning how to run a complex, if small-scale, economy from scratch. There can be no rehearsals; for all the technical and organisational skills they learned in Colomoncagua, nothing there could have prepared them for this.

François, who has been working and living with the community since the refugee camp, agrees. "The economy of Colomoncagua was like no economy in the world – not an economy at all, really. It was completely artificial. The refugees never bought any of the materials for the workshops: aid provided them. But they never really sold anything, either: they used the things they made themselves, or else they were sent overseas and sold through the solidarity committees, never as part of a real market."

Helena, who has been listening quietly at the kitchen door, speaks up. "But the workshops did have two really important functions. First, they were therapeutic: when we were so confined, when we couldn't go anywhere and were constantly under siege from the Honduran military, the workshops gave us something to do. They kept people's spirits up, I think they kept them from going crazy. Then the other thing they did was to teach people all kinds of new skills, new knowledge – because, remember, we were just peasants before the refuge, we knew nothing else. Learning how to make shoes, how to make furniture, how to repair cars, do metalwork, make clothes, even the little poultry and rabbit farms we started up – it all gave us new skills and a new sense of dignity."

There was another aspect to it, too, as Tomás remarks. "The refuge was a great school for us, because that was where we learnt to work in community. There, you didn't work just for yourself or for your family, but for the community. All the work we did was collective, we were united by it. That time in the refuge has been a great help to us; we gained experience in many new things, and we kept on learning and working together right up to the time we came back to El Salvador. The communal life was a very different life, a beautiful life, because we all helped each other."

Paul returns to the question of skills. "It's true that the experience of Colomoncagua certainly produced a unique workforce for this part of the country – probably for the whole country. We've even had businessmen coming up here from the city and taking an interest in us, and that's because this is a special workforce, a highly qualified workforce."

We note that in our tour of the workshops this afternoon, we saw widely differing degrees of apparent success. It looked to us as if some of the workshops might not survive, but that others had possibilities. What determines which ones will become viable and which won't? Are the big orders, like the ones they have had for school desks and for boots, likely to be repeated often enough to keep the workshops going, or are they just a short-term solution while local and regional trade resuscitates?

François replies: "The big problem is that the skills by themselves aren't enough. They have to be relevant to life here – and we've already seen that some things just haven't made sense here, like the knitting workshop; it had to close down months ago."

So the workshops will have to tailor themselves to local needs, the local market, local price structures?

"It's not just the local system they have to mesh into," says François. "During the war, in 1990 and 1991, there was a captive market north of the Torola. but now they've built the bridge, the Community's got to compete with producers and traders from Gotera and San Miguel who've always worked in the capitalist system; and we don't have any experience of marketing. This is a problem for all the northern communities; but it seems more pressing for CSM, because we're producing so much more without having any outlets for it."

Jean says: "This new emphasis on economic development isn't just something we aid agencies have foisted on our project partners, you know! There's been a real change in people's vision of development all over El Salvador. Whether they be popular organisations or communities, everyone's talking about getting a higher technical level, becoming more business-oriented. This isn't the only community trying to become more self-sufficient; these days there is an assumption that economic development means success in the market. It's a real turnaround from the communal ideal that motivated the popular organisations for so long."

Juan José responds: "That's why we think decentralisation is the best solution. We want to phase out the single, centralised structure and make Community organisations totally 'independent' – economically, politically, and socially. The question is: will the Community's organisations manage to survive once their organic economic links with the Community are severed?

"At present all Community structures depend on the central administration, which plans the entire budget. In the future they'll cease to draw their running expenses from a central fund. Instead, they'll calculate the total investment and working capital they'll each need from the central fund to function autonomously. As soon as they start to make a profit, they can begin to make their own repayments on the investment. The Community would simply maintain follow-up and evaluation mechanisms so as to be able to advise them on how to stay afloat."

But, we wonder, doesn't decentralisation really mean privatisation, and the abandonment of everything that made Colomoncagua such an inspiration? – not only to the popular movement in El Salvador, but to us in Europe and North America? Now that 'socialism' has collapsed in Eastern Europe, is there nothing but neoliberal economics to replace it? Might CSM fall into the same trap?

Or is there no alternative? Does CSM have any choice but to embrace market capitalism?

"There's been a lot of debate about this in the FMLN," says Paul. "Many people on the Left in Latin America feel that, whatever the failings of Eastern European socialism and central planning, its fall has left them without a model. We may not like the idea of embracing the market but there's no other model on offer."

"But decentralisation doesn't mean we'll end up with no resources at all for social programmes", says Juan José. "As I said, decentralisation for us means not just sharing out the benefits, the goods, but also the responsibilities, the duties, the rights.

"Although we're moving towards different forms of ownership and different means of production, we still have to preserve the communal project – the basic idea of the communal good, the Community. That will mean retaining some of the Community's infrastructures and enterprises.

"Two different currents of thought seem to be coming out of the discussions: one is the communitarian way of thinking which sees things more or less in the way we saw them in Colomoncagua – that the Community is a single entity and everything in it belongs to it; the other view sees us not so much as a single structure but as a group of people who live together and share the same expectations, the same dreams for a better way, but have very different ideas about how to achieve that. So there has to be a wider view that takes on board both ways of thinking. At the end of the day, we all live in the same place and we share the same history, the same destiny."

*****

The Navajo Indians, says Paul, don't talk of moonlight, but of 'moonwater'. Tonight is awash with it – a nearly full moon, glowing hazily through thin, high cloud. Quebrachos is drenched in this aqueous silver light. Over in the east, fitful sheet lightning flares pale gold against high-piled violet cloud castles. Fireflies switch their tiny dayglo green glimmers on and off like Christmas lights. We need no torches to see our way to the 'little hotel' from the café: the flat tin roofs, the muddy, rutted road, the football pitch and the hills beyond all lie open under moonwater.

Bidding goodnight to Juan José, we comment that changes in the Community of the scope he has been outlining to us seem a very tall order. Juan José agrees, with a laugh. "But of course we don't expect all this to happen overnight. It's a long process which will take at least eight years, till the end of the century – that's why we call it Target 2000."

4
Cleotilde

The ground trembles. We jolt awake. Still completely dark: it must be about three in the morning. Whatever is coming towards us is thundering, and blazing with light. A tank! Reason cuts in: that's over, there aren't any tanks. But for just a moment we have glimpsed the pure terror that must have been the daily companion, for years on end, of the people who refused to leave El Salvador's battle zones.

The roaring and ground-shaking swell in an ominous crescendo. Searchlight beams rake the building, reaching in through every knothole. We scramble up, open the door and look out. The monster is within five yards of the house. Not a tank, but, surging down the narrow mud track between the tiny, ramshackle buildings and the half-tamed vegetation, it might well be one. Its huge headlights throw *film-noir* shadows across the scattered houses. On its yellow flank it bears the circle of blue stars denoting an item of European Community aid. It's the CSM bulldozer, heading for one of the new housing sites in Quebrachos or Los Hatos.

The dragon's passing has woken the entire neighbourhood and the dawn chorus is now in full swing, like a particularly manic rendition of 'Old MacDonald'. Roosters are telling each other the news for miles around, dogs begin to clamour, pigs to snuffle and squeal and rummage. The first drowsy conversations start up as women lull hungry babies, send children off to fetch water, get cooking fires started. Rich hawking and coughing punctuates the soft lilt of voices: respiratory ailments are common here. By a quarter to five, equally bronchitic, the first buses are wheezing and honking up towards Perquín. The day starts early in Morazán.

*****

Quebrachos in the early morning is breathtaking, a water-colour in soft greyish greens and blue-white. From the road you look out upon limitless alternations of mountain and valley, silhouetted by the mist that fills the valley bottoms and is rising dreamily to meet you. By seven, the road is alive with people: groups of schoolchildren, teachers in their pastel uniforms, office workers with bags and books, men and young boys with curved machetes on their way to or from the *milpa* – many have already been at work for two hours.

Our day starts with a visit to Cleotilde, who, as a member of the Reception Committee at Colomoncagua, had acted as our guide during a two-week visit there in 1988. Just a month ago, she opened a little shop in Quebrachos. It's a comfortable, friendly place, something of a social centre, like those corner shops that still survive in rural England. Serving-hatch windows on opposite sides of the room open out onto both the road and the sprawl of houses: hinged at the top, the galvanised iron sheets are propped up on long sticks, creating awnings.

Inside, the shop is tidy and cool. Crammed shelves reach up almost to the ceiling: as well as the expected cigarettes, matches, batteries, torches, pens and pencils, coarse washing powder and bars of soap, there are tins of fruit juice, little gift packs of soap and perfume, small pots of brilliantine for the hair, sticks of cinnamon, even cigars ("The old ladies like a cigar," Cleo smiles, "it's traditional." Kitchen gardens in the past often had a bed of tobacco plants). In the middle of the room are piled boxes and bags of fresh produce: oranges, tomatoes, onions. Biscuits, cakes and tarts for the Salvadorean sweet tooth are brought up daily by a baker from across the Torola. The cash box is a locked drawer in an oddly elegant little side table inlaid with precious woods. In a corner, a short hammock, for sitting in rather than sleeping, hangs among bags of rice, crates of coke, and huge boxes of the universally adored crisps, cheese pops, and corn chips.

Cleo, in grey skirt, striped blouse, and ruched red hairband, presides over all this with pride and a motherly efficiency. It is her newest project, and has only been open for a few weeks.

"I'd been trying to decide what to do, looking at this and that; at one time I'd thought of opening a *pupusería* [shop or stall selling *pupusas*, the national delicacy, a sort of steamed pasty of maize dough filled with spiced mincemeat or cheese]; but in the end I decided that running a shop would be an easier job. I'm not getting any younger, you know, and I'm quite tired of working – but that doesn't mean I want to sit around with my arms folded! I'm a dressmaker by training; but sitting at a machine is hard on the back and shoulders. At some point I might start up a business teaching dressmaking."

The shop is one of a row of little private shops in Quebrachos known as the 'little market'. They all rent their premises from the Community (at a 'symbolic' rent of ¢15 – just over £1 – a month), and they all sell roughly similar wares. How do they hope to survive? People here are learning about small private enterprise the hard way, by trial and error;

learning how to compete in terms of prices, quality and variety of goods, opening hours, quality of service.

Like most if not all the small private shopkeepers, Cleo buys her basic goods wholesale from CODECO, the Community's marketing organisation, which also supplies the Community-owned SuperMontes shops. "They give us prices low enough so that we can sell at the same prices as the SuperMontes ... we make a very little profit, but enough to live on: a fair profit."

Cleo conveys these details sporadically in the intervals between a steady stream of customers. A lively old lady buys eight items one by one, paying for each one as she chooses it – involving eight longwinded transactions in small change – and gossiping in between. It takes her about twenty minutes to amass all she needs, including a final, complimentary biscuit. A child rushes up and rather brusquely demands change of a colón (about 7p). A slow-spoken farmer from somewhere near Perquín buys nothing at all but spends ten minutes discussing comparative food prices in CSM and Perquín and the effect of the VAT recently imposed by the Salvadorean government, which is causing vehement protest nationwide. Another child, waiting for tomatoes to be weighed, stares shyly but steadily at the strange *cheles* (white people) sitting in the corner with notebooks. Cleo folds a sheet of newspaper into a cone for the tomatoes: "Not all the private shops have fruit and vegetables, you know," she says; "in fact mine is one of the few that does, it makes me more competitive."

On average, Cleo's shop brings in ¢200 a day. Out of this she has to buy her goods wholesale, pay her rent on the shop premises, and meet other costs. She employs no one else, and informal arrangements with friends save her some transport costs. Even subtracting her expenses, Cleo can earn a good living compared with the current basic monthly wage at CSM of ¢430.

*****

At the end of the line of huts which house Cleotilde's and the other shops in Quebrachos, the stony track ends in a wide expanse of grass and bare red earth – the football pitch. At this hour it is quiet and peaceful, crossed only by a few children, late for school, and women and young girls carrying garish pink plastic water jars, shaped like a Greek amphora, and bundles of washing, to the communal sinks behind the row of shops. It is hard to imagine that here eleven years ago, on 10 December 1981, helicopters came and went all day, landing troops of the army's Atlacatl

Battalion. Over there they set up their mortars and machine-guns at the edge of the ravine and started firing down at the houses below in the hamlet of La Joya.

Meanwhile, other companies of the Atlacatl battalion had made their way on foot southwards from their initial mustering point in Perquín. From north and west and south they converged on a group of villages which they had decided to punish for allegedly supporting the FMLN guerrillas, and whom they held partly to blame for the humiliation of the new battalion on its first foray into Morazán some nine months earlier. The Atlacatl was the pride of the Salvadorean army, one of the new Rapid Response Battalions, created and trained by US military advisers early in 1981, and specifically designed to fight a modern counter-insurgency war against the guerrillas.

The Atlacatl's targets were the hamlets of La Guacamaya, La Joya and Cerro Pando in the municipality of Meanguera, and Los Toriles. This area had been less affected by the big army 'invasion' of October 1980 when much of the land to the west of the main road had been depopulated, the peasants from San Fernando, Torola, Jocoaitique and Meanguera itself being driven into Villa El Rosario, and then fleeing across the border into Honduras, where they established the refugee camp at Colomoncagua.

*****

On 10 January 1981, almost a year before, the FMLN guerrilla coalition had launched its 'final offensive' against the government. The offensive failed, and in the towns and cities thousands of people who had assisted or sympathised with the FMLN (or its political counterpart the FDR) were left exposed and largely defenceless. Over the next three years many of them were killed by government security forces and death squads, and the leadership of the popular movement (the trade unions, student groups, neighbourhood and church organisations) was virtually destroyed.

One immediate effect of the offensive was to define more clearly areas of the country which were 'under the control of' the FMLN, of which the two largest and most important were Chalatenango in the west and the northern half of Morazán in the east. After the failure of the offensive, urban supporters and sympathisers in danger fled to join the the FMLN in these control zones. Within the zones a substantial proportion of the peasant population offered cover and support to the fighters, and in increasing numbers themselves enlisted to fight.

Until March 1981, the main camp of the FMLN forces in Morazán had been in the village of La Guacamaya, about half an hour's walk from El Mozote, and not more than a couple of hours from the place where Ciudad Segundo Montes stands today. In the first days of that month the Salvadorean army mounted a large operation to encircle the guerrillas, who for some weeks chose to stand their ground, despite being vastly outnumbered. On 24 March hundreds of guerrillas and civilians gathered at the church at El Mozote, to hear Fr Rogelio Ponseele say Mass on the first anniversary of the assassination of Mgr Romero, the hugely popular Archbishop of San Salvador. The service was transmitted by Radio Venceremos, the guerrilla radio station. A few days later the guerrilla forces managed to evade the army and establish a new camp at Ojo de Agua. Soon after that they took Villa El Rosario, and in August they occupied Perquín for ten days.

Early in December 1981, the Salvadorean army launched a much larger offensive against the FMLN guerrillas in Morazán who had moved camp again to El Zapotal, a few miles from La Guacamaya, to the east of the Sapo river. The operation, called Hammer and Anvil, was designed to crush the guerrillas between two large army formations. For the first time large numbers of troops were airlifted in by the new helicopters supplied by the United States. The army, headed by the Atlacatl Battalion under the command of Lt Col Domingo Monterrosa, came very near to succeeding in its objective. By 12 December the FMLN were forced to leave El Zapotal and escape to the west, some of them crossing the Torola river and climbing Mt Cacahuatique. Radio Venceremos was off the air for almost two weeks when they were forced to abandon its transmitter and generator during an army ambush.

*****

A couple of days beforehand, Radio Venceremos had warned of the coming army operation, but the people in El Mozote had believed themselves safe. According to some testimonies, there was a significant number of Protestant evangelicals in the village. Such people would have nothing to do with the guerrillas, were opposed to social activism, and were regarded by the army as reliable (in contrast to the Roman Catholic catechists and Christian base community members, who were assumed to be 'subversives' and supporters of the FMLN).

José Marcos Díaz was a Mozote shopkeeper. He owned quite a substantial, cement block house almost opposite the church. Around the courtyard of this unusual house were various small rooms used as workshops for a training project in crafts such as tailoring and carpentry. José was married to Candelaria, whose cousin, Gloria Romero, is one of the human rights workers in Ciudad Segundo Montes today. Early in December, José was stopped by the army in San Francisco Gotera as he was returning in his truck from San Miguel, where he had gone to buy supplies for his shop. The soldiers warned him that soon no one would be allowed through to El Mozote, because the Atlacatl Battalion was going to start a big operation in the area. José was advised to stock up his shop and to warn people to congregate in El Mozote, where they would be safe: anyone caught in the surrounding area was liable to be killed. José told his neighbours and a large number of peasants from the surrounding area gathered in the village, many of them sleeping in José's house.

As well as the Hammer and Anvil operation, the Salvadorean army initiated Operation Rescue. In some US adviser's textbook, this may have been presented as an operation about 'rescuing' civilians from guerrilla influence. But it was interpreted by the Salvadorean military in much the same way as the priests who travelled with the Spanish conquerors and consigned Indians to the flames to hasten their salvation. Whatever its origin, this counter-insurgency operation will always be remembered by the name of the village at the epicentre of the encirclement – El Mozote.

5
El Mozote

Today important visitors are expected at the Cultural Centre. Three long tables have been placed end-to-end and neatly covered with white sheets. A vase of flowers stands rather incongruously in the middle, and banners strung from the roof-beams read 'To bring Justice is to build Peace: Welcome to the Truth Commission. CDHM' and 'Walking in the path of Truth we will open up the road to Justice'. From behind the kitchen come the sounds of the music group, Conjunto Morazán, tuning up. Half a dozen ONUSAL officers in dark glasses and neatly pressed olive green uniforms are standing about in self-important contrast to the gathering crowd of people from the Community.

Gloria and Mercedes from CDHM look anxious. They have been up since first light, preparing to receive the visit of the Truth Commission, which arrived in the country yesterday. A large contingent from the Community, including the Conjunto, went yesterday to San Salvador to greet them, but the flight times were changed, and the welcoming ceremony in the capital had to be abandoned. Established under the terms of the Peace Accords, the Commission consists of three eminent international figures, headed by Belisario Betancur, the former president of Colombia. Their mandate is to investigate 'those serious acts of violence which have occurred since 1980, about which the public urgently needs to know the truth'. They have come to Morazán, on the second day of their stay, to visit the site of the massacre at El Mozote, the worst single incident of the twelve-year war. It is a gesture whose significance will not be lost on the armed forces, who have always denied that any massacre took place.

After a long delay, the drone of an engine is heard, approaching fast from the direction of Quebrachos. After circling the hilltop several times, a gleaming white UN helicopter touches down in the car-park beside the Cultural Centre, sending blinding swirls of dust into the waiting crowd. The door slides open and an official emerges, clutching an armful of papers, which are instantly torn from his grasp by the slip-stream of the rotors and tossed into the air before disappearing over the edge of the plateau and dancing away down towards Los Hatos. After disembarking its passengers without turning off its engines, the helicopter lifts off again, and a second, identical machine touches down, to disgorge the distinguished visitors. The Conjunto strikes up a tune of welcome, but the music is lost amidst the clatter of the rotors.

The guests are seated at the long table and women serve coffee and cakes. Mercedes gives a short speech of welcome, and then Belisario Betancur announces the purpose of the mission. They have come, he stresses, to listen to everyone, to be objective, to hear all the testimony, to discover the truth. They have little time and a busy schedule, he explains, but they had thought it important to come to Morazán.

A woman sitting at the table beside Mercedes asks to speak. This is Rufina Amaya, who survived the massacre at El Mozote, managed to reach Colomoncagua and returned to Morazán with the other refugees in 1980. With the Commission's agreement she begins calmly and confidently to give her testimony. She speaks clearly and without hesitation for perhaps ten minutes, but as she talks, the Commission members begin to fidget and consult their watches. Eventually, the President intervenes: they are sorry, but they cannot stay, they are late for another appointment in San Salvador. He promises that Rufina's testimony will be recorded in full by the secretariat they will establish in San Salvador.

The helicopters return and the men in suits depart. Two members of the Commission staff remain behind to talk to Rufina and Mercedes. Afterwards we ask Rufina why she isn't angry at being treated in this way. She shrugs: "They came. That's what matters."

*****

From the bombed-out ruins of Arambala a rough dirt road heads east towards Joateca. After a couple of miles a crude wooden board marks the turn-off. A deeply rutted track winds amongst low, scrubby trees, whose contorted trunks veer away from the bouncing jeep, seeming to mock as the wheels bounce off hidden boulders to mire themselves in the reddish clay. Every now and then there are the remains of a house, empty, roofless, the unprotected adobe walls slowly dissolving back to dust and mud under the alternation of rain and drought, and the prying feelers of rampant undergrowth. Eventually the track shakes off the trees and emerges onto a level area open to the sky, with grass fresh-cropped, and almost the aspect of parkland. A little further on is a village square, or rather what must once have been one. Apart from half a dozen cows the place is deserted. In a countryside usually raucous with the crowing of cocks and the shouts and cries of children, the stillness and silence is unnatural.

To the left, in front of the ruined shell of a single-storey cement-block building is an open area perhaps 50 yards wide. In the middle stands a monument: four figures, a man and a woman with a child on either side, stand in line, holding hands. Cut out of beaten copper sheet, not moulded or sculpted; acid-etched or annealed in some way, without a trace of verdigris. There is no plinth: the figures stand among stones on the open ground amidst grass and weeds. They are small, perhaps only about four feet high – but perfectly proportioned to the ruins. Even from very close to they appear dark and featureless, yet the outlines are detailed, full of life and movement, leaning slightly as though about to run forwards, the tension in their arms and clasped hands suggesting unity in the face of hope or fear. The effect is extraordinary: rather than images of live people, these are the voids left when living people are suddenly taken away, killed or disappeared, like those terrible human shadows etched into walls in Hiroshima.

A simple bronze plaque reads:

> THEY ARE NOT DEAD; THEY ARE WITH US,
> WITH YOU AND WITH ALL HUMANITY.
>
> EL MOZOTE, 11 DECEMBER 1981

*****

"Mozote was a really pretty place. All that level ground, where there were small trees in those days, mostly apples. Maybe it wasn't the trees which made it pretty so much as the grass. The whole area was grassy, almost like a lawn, very green and level. The climate is nice and cool there, as well. Nowadays it looks ugly, because of the scrub everywhere."

Don Virgilio, who works in the bookshop at San Luis, remembers what Mozote was like before. But for him, as for almost everyone in Ciudad Segundo Montes, it holds other memories as well:

"It must have been very moving for you, seeing the monument there. But for those of us who knew the place well before, there is so much more... so many people. They killed relatives of mine there: my sister's daughter Rosa, with her two children, a little girl of about six and a one-month-old baby boy. They killed one of my aunts, who was

Monument to those killed in the
El Mozote massacre, 1981

Mike George

over 60; and another aunt of 52. They killed her son who was 20 and his wife who was 19, together with their two children. They were killed in the big house there, the one that belonged to that lad Marcos Díaz. A lot of people had taken refuge there, thinking that if they stuck together and stayed put, nothing would happen to them, because they were innocent, they weren't involved. They didn't want to run away, but they were killed anyway. Really all those people who died were innocent."

One person is known for sure to have witnessed the massacre itself and survived – Rufina. This is the testimony she started to give to the Truth Commission, and has given so many times to human rights workers from all over the world:

"A lot of Salvadorean army soldiers came into the village and dragged us out of the houses. They made us lie face down in the street – men, women and children all lumped together. Then they shut us up in the houses again. This was around six o'clock in the afternoon on December 10. They threatened to shoot us if we so much as stirred outside. The whole village was shut up indoors.

At around 4.00am the next day they brought us outside again, separated us into two lines in the village square, one for men and one for women. At 7.00am a helicopter landed in the village, and some military disembarked. They ordered us women to be shut in the house of Alfredo Márquez and the house of Benita Díaz, and the men were all shut up in the church. The helicopter took off again and disappeared. The soldiers came into the house where we were, threatening us with knives and rifles, asking what we were doing there and accusing us of collaborating with the guerrillas. There were a lot of us there and we all had our children. They put knives to our throats. We were in such a state all we could do was cry and pray. Most of the soldiers then disappeared, leaving a handful on guard. A few moments later we heard the screams of the men from inside the church. We said to each other, 'Maybe they're killing them.' I had my four children with me, the baby in my arms and the other three clinging to my skirt. I managed to get up on a bench and look through the window to see what was happening to the men in the church opposite. I could see that they had blindfolded and tied them hand and foot. They were all lying face down on the church floor, almost in one pile. The soldiers were running up and down over their backs, beating them with their rifle butts.

Annual commemoration of El Mozote massacre. 'Nine years after the cruel massacre, we demand justice and punishment of the El Mozote murderers.'

ESCHR

I couldn't tear myself away, but stayed there watching. So I saw when they started to bring them out in groups to kill them beside the convent. Some they beheaded, others they machine-gunned. I saw them shoot my husband, the father of my children, and others I knew, some of them my cousins. I turned to the women and said 'They're shooting the men', so all the women tried to look through the windows to see, crying, and screaming out to the soldiers not to kill them, but to take them instead to San Miguel or to Gotera. They were begging, but the soldiers wouldn't listen. I just sat down with my four children on the bench to cry and to pray to God.

One of the women said, 'They've almost finished killing them; there are hardly any men left now.' Then the soldiers came over and started to lead the women out. First they took the young girls away to the hillside, their mothers crying and hanging onto their daughters' hands. So the soldiers beat the mothers off with their rifle butts, knocking them down onto the benches. Then they took the mothers, the dumb and the blind, and the women who were crying most. Again, they took them out a group at a time, to kill them. No one came back. The children were left behind, a lot of children, on the floor, lots of them really small, some babies only a few days old, naked on the floor.

They took me out at around five in the afternoon. There were only a few women left by then. I had been sitting there all that time, with my baby on my lap, praying to God to look after us. The soldiers came up to me and said 'Get up, you. We're taking you out to set you free, and let you go home.' They grabbed hold of me and made me stand up, but I didn't want to let go of the baby. Two soldiers grabbed her and took her away from me. They grabbed me by the neck and tried to take the holy medallion I was wearing. I didn't let them, but dodged sideways and went to the back of the line of women they were taking out to kill. They took us out in single file, towards the house of Israel Márquez. We could see that there were dead bodies in the house already, and that our group would be taken in and we would be killed there too. So when the women saw the bodies they shrank back, grabbing hold of each other, and crying out to the soldiers not to kill them. 'Take us away, to Gotera if you like, but don't kill us.' The soldiers replied 'Don't cry. Look: here comes the Devil to take you away.' That's what they said. Of course that made the women cry and scream even more desperately.

Then I started to say the Lord's Prayer. As I was praying, on my knees, I edged sideways and managed to get behind the branch of an apple tree, pulling the branch downwards so that it would cover my feet, and hiding my face behind the leaves. It was a very small tree but I managed to stay there. The soldiers were busy with the mothers, who had all grabbed hold of one another in their grief, and they didn't notice that I had hidden. Also, it was beginning to get dark. So they finished killing that group and went to bring out another.

By six o'clock night was falling. When they had finished killing the women, the soldiers set fire to the bodies. Some of the women had taken their children with them, while others had remained behind, shut in. Just by the bonfire of corpses a child cried out, and one of the soldiers said, "Why don't you kill that one?" There was a burst of gunfire, and the child didn't cry out anymore. I was desperate, because I'd left behind my four children who'd been locked up.
At about eleven that night I could hear cries from the children, calling for their mothers. The soldiers were killing them too. They were hanging them, cutting their throats. I couldn't hear any shots, just the children's screams.

Finally I managed to get away. I didn't want to go, because I could still hear the children crying. I had this idea they might take them with them. I left my hiding place, in the shadows of the fires the soldiers had lit. There were some animals running around in panic – some dogs, a couple of calves. I hid among them, between their legs, and got away. I was terribly upset, because I'd left my children behind: a boy aged nine, a girl aged five, one aged three and the baby who was just eight months. I still couldn't believe they'd kill them.

I got away and made for a place where there was nothing, no people, nothing. Everyone in that area – round La Joya, Cerro Pando and Los Toriles – had been killed. All the people were dead. I wandered on my own for a week, without meeting a living soul. Then, in a ravine, I came across a family and I stayed with them until I went to Colomoncagua, in early 1982.

I was the only survivor of El Mozote. My four children and my husband were among those who were killed."

Juan Bautista, the lay-preacher at Quebrachos, remembers:

"After the massacre I went to look for my mother. She was one of those killed there. I couldn't bring myself to enter the village, the stench of death was so terrible. So after that I fled to Honduras, hiding out by day and crossing the frontier at night, because the army were still all over the area, in Perquín and in Jocoaitique."

The report of *Tutela Legal*, the human rights organisation of the Archdiocese of San Salvador, lists 393 identified individuals known to have died in El Mozote itself, and many others in the surrounding villages. In all, 794 people are known to have died. There were probably many more.

Today, only the half-dozen houses in Mozote which had cement-block walls remain clearly visible. Most of the dwellings and the church were built of adobe and are slowly melting back into the earth. Not a single building has a roof. No one lives in Mozote. It is a graveyard.

6
Arambala Reborn

To anyone coming from a city in the developed world – or even from San Salvador – northern Morazán seems an Eden innocent of road traffic. Around one vehicle every five minutes travels the five kilometres of paved road between San Luis and Quebrachos during the day; more during the community's 'rush hours' at the beginning and end of the working day or during the flurry of market or feast day; far fewer at night.

Now imagine this road in the mid-1980s, silent and abandoned. No cars, no jeeps, no battered pickups, no buses, no bicycles, no ox-carts on the bomb-pitted, weed-choked tarmac. No military traffic either – at least not on the ground – except for a few patched-up or made-over FMLN vehicles. After the FMLN blew up the bridge over the Torola on the Perquín road on 17 January 1983, leaving the army's Ramón Belloso battalion encircled in Perquín, it was next to impossible for heavy artillery or armoured vehicles to cross into northern Morazán, especially during the rainy 'winter' months.

Today, with the new bridge in place, northern Morazán is easily accessible. Bomb-craters and neglect aside, the road as far north as Perquín is a well-engineered two-lane highway. Beyond, it is unpaved, though graded and gravelled as far as San Fernando, about the only visible evidence so far of a returning government presence. All other roads in the zone are just dirt tracks which smarten themselves up into cobbled streets as they approach a village. It is these age-old roads that beckon you out from the edges of villages like Meanguera or Jocoaitique or Arambala. Tree-shaded and half overgrown with grass, these roads were designed for ox-carts and sauntering mules. More than anything else, they hint at the quiet rhythms of a now-vanished rural life.

Although vehicles of all kinds are seen in northern Morazán these days, their numbers are so small that it is possible to get to know most of the 'regulars' within a week. The new white ONUSAL jeeps, dashing about self-importantly, with their air-conditioning and their in-car radiophones, are the pinnacle of luxury; high-sided, bronchitic old lorries and clapped-out pickups laden to the gunwales with people and produce are the norm. The community owns a few cars, and one or two foreign workers have acquired motorcycles. Private cars are very rare at CSM, although one young war-disabled man earns his living by driving people

Arambala's grocery shop   Jenny Matthews

and goods around in his daffodil-yellow pickup, its flatbed modified for
passengers by the addition of an ornate wrought-iron safety frame. Most
other cars on the road are driven by visitors, increasingly tourists and
Salvadorean daytrippers up from San Miguel or even San Salvador.

The refugees' return to Morazán and the reopening of the north via
the new bridge gave local bus companies several thousand potential new
customers. Two San Miguel-based bus companies were given the
franchise to run the routes in northern Morazán. The new bus routes were
a mixed blessing, however, for the bus companies soon began charging
higher fares north of the Torola than south of it. Not surprisingly, this
aroused indignation in the north and for some time PADECOMSM (the
organisation of communities in Morazán) and the FMLN maintained a
boycott of the commercial buses, occasionally blocking the road to
prevent them from passing. In the meantime, local traders and lorry-
drivers took up the slack in transport, sometimes charging their passengers
a fare. A few lorries and pickups now operate almost exclusively as buses.

The commercial buses are now back in operation, but disputes about
pricing continue. Some of the women simply refuse to pay the higher fare,
saying they've only brought one colón with them. The bus companies,

aware that they are on fragile ground, with increasing competition, are usually obliged to back down. Ciudad Segundo Montes has one bus of its own, a bright yellow American schoolbus, donated by a solidarity group who drove it down from Colorado loaded with gifts. It makes a regular round-trip to the various settlements.The service is far from regular, however, as breakdowns are frequent and for weeks at a time the vehicle sits in the Community's garage, waiting for spare parts to arrive.

*****

Arambala lies a couple of miles up a stony track that forks east off the tarmac road about half way between Ciudad Segundo Montes and Perquín. Once a small town, with a discernible grid of streets, eight or ten blocks, and a wide grassy main square some 150 yards across, it now has not a single building intact. A line of what must once have been shops is gutted and roofless. Of the church, only the square, white tower remains, with a curious egg-like dome over the centre of the open bell-floor, and a couple of arches. As so often in El Salvador, the swift growth of tropical vegetation soon softens the harsh lines of shattered walls and piles of rubble, while torrential rains wash away the scars of fire. Arambala looks placid and peaceful.

Someone has planted new saplings in the square and surrounded each one with a protective ring of sticks. They look incongruous amidst the ruins, as though transplanted from the parkland surrounding an English country house. In the gaps between the old houses one or two wooden huts have been erected, one of them beside the ruins of the church providing a makeshift chapel. Elsewhere corrugated iron roofs have gone up where once there were red clay tiles. In the ruins of the church a teacher is conducting a class with some thirty children sitting on improvised wooden benches. All of these are tokens of new life returning to the community.

In the only building fronting the square which is more or less intact, we find María del Transito Hernández. We talk as she moves around the large front room which doubles as kitchen, living room and simple store. Children and chickens wander in and out. María and her family were refugees in Colomoncagua, and lived in San Luis after the repatriation. But the family came from Arambala, and her mother and sisters had already returned to repopulate the town.

"My husband and I decided that we would come back here too. It was our own decision, but PADECOMSM put forward a proposal [to the leadership of CSM]. They wanted us to come back to work in the committee here. So that's what we did. It was too far for him to be going home to Ciudad Segundo Montes every day, so we decided to bring the whole family, and we started working here, with the PADECOMSM committee who were getting things moving here in Arambala.

It wasn't easy: there's still no drinking water here. We have to go and fetch water from the hill. The only water is down at the bath-house. No one has piped water in their houses. We're just starting to get the place organised again, setting up the school, the chapel, and so on. The school's up and running now, with the help of some [unqualified] community teachers, but four months ago we managed to get an official teacher supplied by the Ministry of Education. At the moment we only go up to second grade. Before the war they taught up to sixth grade here, but we haven't got enough teachers now, and the classrooms were all destroyed in the bombing.

The only things we brought with us from Ciudad Segundo Montes were the materials to rebuild our house. We haven't had any other direct help from them. We have more to do with PADECOMSM, which works with all the communities of the northern zone. My husband is one of the leaders – he's in charge of the cooperatives; and I'm the secretary for education, representing the education workers on the executive committee. If we need something for one of the schools, I bring it up at a committee meeting, and if it's agreed, they have to go and get whatever they need from the PADECOMSM office there in Perquín. 16 July is the feast of the virgin, Carmen, our patron saint, and this year we organised a proper fiesta. We had a procession and carried an image of the virgin round all the streets of Arambala. Then Fr Rogelio said mass in the little wooden chapel we've built alongside the ruins of the church. We had fireworks, and a dance in the evening, with live music, which went on until two in the morning. Lots of people came.

I think more people will come back to live here. There are a lot of people coming here now to work, to clear the land, rebuild, get a roof back up, and see how things are before deciding to bring their families back to live here."

*****

Most people in Ciudad Segundo Montes dream of returning 'some day' to where they lived before the war, and where many of their families had land. Only a quarter of the families originate from Meanguera, the municipality in which CSM itself is situated. The rest are from Torola, Gualococti (a few miles south-west of the Community, across the Torola river), Cacaopera, Jocoaitique, Joateca, Osicala, San Fernando, Arambala, and Perquín. Although all of these places are less than fifteen miles from CSM, it can take the best part of a day to reach some of them, with roads (except for the main road) poor to atrocious, and buses scarce or non-existent.

Jocoaitique, only about half an hour's walk from Quebrachos, lies in a valley just off the main road to Perquín. The Perquín buses stop there, and CSM's own bus goes there twice a day, when it's not off the road for repairs. People say it was once the prettiest village in northern Morazán, and although it did not escape severe war damage, it still has a threadbare chocolate-box charm. One person who has returned there is José Clemente Carrillo, who works at the CSM Garage:

> "When we came back to this area in 1989, we found hardly anyone here at all. There'd been people in Perquín all through the war, but in Jocoaitique there were only about four or five families left. I've just gone back to live there with my family. We still belong to the Community, though, and I come here to work every day."

Distance is a crucial factor. Two teachers in the Community, Fidelina and José, come from Torola:

> "A lot of people are talking about going, but they want to remain members of the Community. 'I want to go home', they say, 'but I still want to belong to Ciudad Segundo Montes'. They want to go back to work their land, but they want to stay here as well. Of course they can't do both, not if their land is any distance away. Torola is a good four hours walk from here. People aren't drifting away individually. They can't. In our hamlet, for instance, there's nothing, not a house standing.What we tell people is that they ought to think twice before going. There won't be a health clinic, there won't be schools, there won't be drinking water."

Without the agreement and help of the CSM leaders, it is very hard for people to leave the Community. We hear rumours several times that people have been refused permission to take building materials with them, and that this has led to a row between CSM and PADECOMSM.

If any substantial number choose to return to their former place of residence, it will make a considerable dent in the population of CSM. Will the Community itself remain viable? Fr Rogelio Ponseele, who spent the war years in this area, accompanying the FMLN and ministering to the gradually re-emergent civilian population, takes a dispassionate view:

"I've noticed recently that people are taking it more calmly, as though they have managed to reconcile several different things: on the one hand to continue building a community which is going to survive in this area, and which is going to be a model of development; and on the other to accept that there will be people who go back to their own place, who settle elsewhere and try to earn a living there."

*****

Ciudad Segundo Montes has made one conscious attempt to found a colony. Some land was obtained at Lempa Mar, on the fertile coastal plain in Usulután, about sixty miles south of the Community. Sixty families went there to build a community more or less from scratch, and are living in very uncomfortable conditions in temporary housing and plagued by mosquitoes and bad water.

The plan, apparently, was intended to resolve CSM's chronic deficit in grain production. The community at Lempa Mar would grow maize and rice on their flat, fertile and well-irrigated fields, and exchange them for bricks, tiles, clothing and other semi-industrial products exported from CSM. The experiment was not a success. The costs and difficulty of transporting goods between the two places more than wiped out any commercial advantage and the people of Lempa Mar came to believe that they were being used as a milch cow.

Juan José is now adamant that CSM hasn't the resources to repopulate more distant places:

"If we really want to see our own municipality develop, we have to stay here. There's no point in trying to repopulate another municipality. If you're going to repopulate, you need a well-defined plan. You need to put in a road, for example, a school, a clinic, those kinds of things. I think our original hunch was right. If we don't promote repopulation elsewhere, it won't happen, because it's really very difficult for people to go off and remake their lives under their own steam."

7
Coming Home

Next morning we are sitting in the Cultural Centre, chatting to Gloria Romero from the Community's Human Rights Committee. We remark that almost everyone we talk to in Ciudad Segundo Montes still has vivid memories of the repatriation – their decision to return *en masse* to their country after nearly ten years of living in exile in Honduras. Gloria volunteers to tell us the story.

When the first repatriations took place in 1987 from Mesa Grande (a refugee camp also in Honduras), the refugees at Colomoncagua had been adamant that they would not return to Morazán while the war was still raging. What changed their minds, we ask?

> "We were all very clear about it," Gloria recalls. "The war was still going on, and the repression was much worse than in previous years. But in 1988 the foreign agencies working with the refugees met in Guatemala and came up with three alternatives for us: to repatriate individually to El Salvador; to be relocated to a third country; or to become nationals of the country where we were living as refugees. What were we do to? We discussed all three points with each sector in the Community and we canvassed everyone's opinion; we all agreed on the first alternative, which was repatriation as a community to El Salvador, despite the continuing repression. We felt that was the only way we'd be able to carry on the projects we'd worked so hard to develop during those years in Honduras."

The refugee leadership sent a letter to CIREFCA, the committee of foreign agencies, formally proposing a collective repatriation. The 1,500 refugees at nearby San Antonio followed suit shortly afterwards. But months of negotiation were to precede the departure. The refugees set a number of conditions: they should be allowed to repatriate collectively to the place they had chosen, taking all their personal and communal belongings with them; they should have the right to continued international accompaniment and the aid and support of international non-governmental organisations; and they should all be issued with Salvadorean identity documents before the return. They also asked the governments and armed forces of both countries to let them open a direct road from Colomoncagua to San Fernando – which meant upgrading the existing mule-trail so that it could carry wheeled vehicles.

Unpacking the contents of Colomoncagua refugee camp. ESCHR
Every last plank of wood was taken back to El Salvador.

While the Honduran authorities were only too glad to be rid of the refugees, their Salvadorean counterparts were not eager to have them back.

"The government didn't like the idea at all," Gloria laughs. "They knew we were going to come back as a community and continue with our projects. But, despite government opposition, the CIREFCA proposals still presented us with the possibility of returning to El Salvador. They'd opened a door for us... So we thought, 'Well, let's go, if we're going, right?' And we set a date."

That date was 15 November. But on 11 November the FMLN embarked on a major offensive. It was the perfect excuse for the Salvadorean government to veto the repatriation. The United Nations High Commission for Refugees (UNHCR) had formally decided, after the tense and confrontational repatriations from Mesa Grande in 1987 and 1988, that it would not support future repatriations without the formal approval of the two governments concerned, and insisted on postponement. Meanwhile, the process of issuing temporary identity documents to the refugees had not begun until 30 October and was averaging only 150 a day, not nearly fast enough to get everyone documented by the deadline. And the road-building was behind schedule.

But the refugees had no intention of waiting. While the leaders talked, the people began to dismantle the camp. Everything, down to the last nail, was to come back to El Salvador for re-use. As well as packing up the communal property – the fabric of the dismantled buildings, school and clinic equipment, workshop materials, machinery, tools, furniture – a wooden box was made for each person in Colomoncagua to bring back their personal belongings. "So," says Gloria, "we had no alternative but to leave as soon as possible, offensive or no offensive. Some of the houses had already been taken down, the infrastructure had been dismantled, and people had stopped working in the workshops. What else were we to do?"

Gloria also acknowledges that in some ways the FMLN offensive was in their favour:

"We knew the army would have to concentrate their forces in the areas where they were under attack, like San Salvador, and that's just what they did. We realised that with the offensive going on, the army... might turn against the civilian population, with bombings and so on, which was what they normally did; but we weren't going back on our decision."

*****

While we have been talking, Cleotilde has joined us, and sits gently bouncing a friend's fretful toddler on her lap. She is among the people waiting for documents, and remarks wryly that we could be here all day. She tells us how, impatient at the delay in the repatriation, the refugees seized the initiative. "We decided that if they weren't going to give us any transport, we didn't need lorries to travel. We had our feet, and we had our will to return, on foot if need be. After all, we hadn't had any transport when we came to Honduras in the first place!" On 18 November a group of about 700 people set off on foot, against the advice of UNHCR and without transport backup, carrying only a little food and tools to begin making the road between San Fernando and the border.

They gave no notice to anyone except PADECOMSM (the organisation representing Morazán's northern communities), which had helped them choose the repatriation site. "No one at UNHCR or the other organisations knew about the departure of the first group from Colomoncagua," says Gloria. "Only the Community itself knew. It had all been prepared on the spur of the moment."

Their exit from the camp took their Honduran guards by surprise.

"At the checkpoint halfway between Colo [the camp] and the village, the Honduran soldiers refused to let us through. But we all marched past, shouting slogans and telling them why the people were moving out, and thanking the Honduran inhabitants of Colomoncagua village. We had banners and placards to explain what we were doing and where we were going."

After holding them up for three hours at the checkpoint, the Honduran military tried – unsuccessfully – to divert them round Colomoncagua village:

"When we got to the village, more hassle! There was the army waiting on both sides. But our people just carried on in two columns, looking straight ahead. There were people standing about watching and wondering whether we were coming to demonstrate in the village or what. Then suddenly UNHCR turned up, and everyone realised we were on our way [back home]. That caused a real uproar; UNHCR didn't know what to do."

In the end, after some argument, UNHCR decided to go to the border with the refugees without actually participating in the convoy. Salvadorean immigration officials tried to stop them and check their documentation at the border, but the refugees walked straight past them and on to San Fernando, where they were met by PADECOMSM vehicles. From there they continued on to Perquín.

Cleotilde, who was in the 18 November group, takes up the story on the Salvadorean side, recounting how the group was met by people from the nearby communities, and how they were welcomed with food and festivities by a delegation from the FMLN. The returning refugees had seen uniformed fighters shadowing their progress from the border, but only once they were well inside El Salvador did they realise who they were:

"When we got to the edge of the village they spoke to us... and we could see their insignia, because they always wear an FMLN bandanna, and so we knew they weren't the army – and also because of the way they greeted us, kindly and cheerfully, hugging people."

After staying the night at Perquín, the group went on to Jocoaitique, where they established a base for the preliminary work on the new settlement:

"We organised ourselves into teams to work on the places where the settlements were going to be: clearing undergrowth, putting up fences, making roads. Those who were educators worked with the children, giving classes, and those of us who'd been in the workshops repaired and made things; other people were organised in kitchens, cooking for the people. About twenty teams of men, women and boys made that road from San Fernando to Colomoncagua."

Cleo paints a vivid picture of the joys and sorrows of the return.

"The children ran about all over the place, happy as larks, picking any fruit they wanted – in the refuge you couldn't just eat fruit when you fancied it: if the agencies didn't bring it to us we didn't get it... Coming back, we were full of memories, as we walked along the roads... Seeing people milking cows was a real surprise for the children. 'Why are they pulling at the cow's teats?' they asked. You see, there weren't any cattle in Colo. And when we were looking at the places that had been bombed out, the children would pick up bits and pieces and we had to explain that they'd come from bombs the planes had dropped."

Almost immediately after this group's return, the Salvadorean government suspended 'indefinitely' any agreement on the repatriation. On 7 December the refugees let it be known that another group would return two days later. UNHCR was still refusing to offer active support such as transport until it had the Salvadorean government's formal agreement to the repatriation, so the refugees organised the provision of vehicles themselves and quietly obtained authorisation from Col. Abraham Turcios, head of the Honduran government refugee agency, to bring them into the camps for loading. Five hundred people and 26 lorries left the camp on 9 December, accompanied by international observers, aid agency staff and journalists. "They came to the border in lorries", says Cleo, "and we met them with lorries arranged by the communities of northern Morazán." The transfer of people and materials had begun in earnest. By 29 January six groups had repatriated, and by 27 February all 8,400 refugees had returned to El Salvador. The government and UNHCR accepted a *fait accompli* and gave official permission for the last groups to return.

The main problem now, Gloria remarks, is government sluggishness in issuing documents – identity cards, land titles, etc. Hardly anyone in the Community has them, and without them their lives are severely restricted. Although the Peace Accords have brought an end to active military harassment, it's clear the government dislikes and distrusts the Community as much as it did on the day the first group of returnees – dogged, wary, but jubilant – tramped home to Morazán.

8
Captured

Just below the Cultural Centre is a group of square, cream-coloured huts with red-tiled roofs which house the External Relations Office, the visitors' guesthouse and the offices of the Committee for Human Rights in Morazán, CDHM, where Gloria works. In one room a young man, Toribio, is busy transcribing tapes of testimony and wrestling with a word-processor.

CDHM was established in March 1990, Gloria explains, one month after the repatriation to Ciudad Segundo Montes was complete. At the time there was still an atmosphere of extreme tension, following the FMLN's major offensive in November 1989 which had brought the war to the heart of the country's capital city and come close to defeating the Salvadorean army. While northern Morazán remained an FMLN controlled zone, there were frequent army incursions, and the inhabitants of Ciudad Segundo Montes, much the largest concentration of civilians in the area, were an obvious target for army suspicion and reprisals.

Many Community members were 'captured', *capturado* – a word with a very precise connotation difficult to convey in English. The word 'arrest' suggests a whole framework of legality with legal warrants, cautions, formal charges, rights to silence and to legal representation, *habeas corpus*, etc. – entirely absent in El Salvador even in peacetime. The word 'caught' suggests guilty people on the run. People who get 'captured' by the armed forces in El Salvador are for the most part innocent civilians asleep in their beds, waiting at the bus stop, going shopping or coming out of church. No warrant or legal document exists. No one is told where the prisoner is taken. Unless there are witnesses, the person simply disappears, for hours or days, sometimes for ever.

When it was first established, the Human Rights Committee's job was, as Gloria explains:

"To begin documenting the first cases of people being captured straightaway. In March, April and May 1990, the first few months after our return to Morazán, there was a spate of captures by government soldiers. We secured the release of most of these people with the support and determination of the whole of the Community. Our Committee had to organise people and transport them to San Francisco Gotera to protest in front of the army barracks where our people were being held. We did it again and again, sometimes mobilising up to 1,000 people. We've been successful: out of over 65 captures in the two and a half years we've been here, we've finally secured the release of every single one...

One of our biggest problems from the time we repatriated up until the Peace Accords were the checkpoints on the road. The army put up five of these between San Francisco Gotera and the Community. The one nearest to us was at the Osicala turn-off, just across the Bridge... The checkpoints set back our development plan considerably, especially the house-building programme, because we couldn't get materials through, and the workers would be sitting around waiting for the stuff to arrive. At one time the army even had a list of 'restricted materials' which were not allowed to reach the Community: mainly tools, batteries, and fuel for the motors in the workshops and the Community's vehicles. Of course, they claimed we were passing on these things to the guerrillas."

Gloria shows us a file of monthly human rights summaries and testimonies. They give a flavour of the permanent climate of fear in which the 'repatriates', the inhabitants of Ciudad Segundo Montes, lived during the period between their return to Morazán and the signing of the Peace Accords.

One of the most dramatic incidents occurred on 12 January 1991. A lorry belonging to the Community was on its way home with drums of diesel oil and fresh food for the cafeterias when it was stopped at a checkpoint on the outskirts of San Francisco Gotera. The driver, Efigénio Márquez Vigil, was dragged off to the barracks where he was stripped, blindfolded and interrogated. When the news reached Ciudad Segundo Montes, a group of 130 people went down to Gotera and maintained a peaceful picket outside the barracks all night long.

Early the following morning another 180 people from Ciudad Segundo Montes joined the others in the town. They were soon surrounded by a military cordon; the soldiers spread a yellow powder on the ground which caused vomiting and breathing difficulties. Their eyes still streaming, the people regrouped about one block away from the crossroads. They washed themselves with water brought out by the inhabitants of the town. Soldiers chased some of them to a point about two blocks away from the edge of town, threatening to capture them and throwing more of the powder.

Soon afterwards Efigénio and the lorry were released without charge, and everyone returned to the Community.

The Community protests: a march in San Francisco Gotera, the local garrison town. 'We demand the immediate removal of military checkpoints.'   ESCHR

*****

Ordinary people in the town were amazed: they had never seen unarmed people defying the army in this way. While many were suspicious of the Community, a good few were heartened and helped the CSM protesters as much as they dared: passing food and water to them and taking them into their houses.

Eventually, according to Gloria, Colonel Linares conceded that materials essential to the Community could be taken freely through the checkpoints, provided that he was notified in advance by telephone, but in practice this was a farce, as the Colonel was always 'busy' or 'out'.

"After that we just brought the lorries through, without permits and without phoning. They often stopped the vehicles, but in the end we managed to break the blockade. It helped not just the people of Ciudad Segundo Montes, but the other communities in northern Morazán as well."

The checkpoints gradually lightened as the war abated, although they did not finally disappear until after the ceasefire. The opening of the Torola bridge in June 1990 and the immediate boost in local trade across the river had made them look even more anachronistic. But the army was still capable of mounting a 'show' for punitive or propaganda purposes. On 11 December 1991, for instance, the tenth anniversary of the El Mozote massacre, they set up as many as fourteen checkpoints between the Cuscatlán bridge on the Panamerican Highway and Perquín, obstructing delegations to El Mozote from the Jesuit Central American University and international organisations.

Much of the improvement was the result of the UN observer contingent, ONUSAL, established under the San José Accord of 26 July 1990. ONUSAL was empowered to go anywhere in the country and visit any government facility without notice. This brought it into head-on collision with the army's restrictions on freedom of movement, which had no legal or constitutional basis. ONUSAL representatives often found themselves intervening on behalf of local people and humanitarian agencies, either with the soldiers manning the roadblocks or with their superiors in the local detachment or brigade headquarters.

*****

A slim woman with light brown hair and freckles has come into the cramped office. This is Mercedes, the coordinator of the Human Rights Committee. "Since the Peace Accords", she says, "a lot has changed. The repression has really stopped. That's been the big achievement for us, for the people of El Salvador." Gloria is not quite so sure: "There are still problems, though. We've seen a number of robberies and assaults on members of the Community, which might be mistaken for common crimes. But we know that the people who commit these assaults come from the army battalions."

She cites an attack in March this year on a group from the Communal Services organisation of the Community who had gone to San Miguel to cash a cheque for ¢60,220 (about £4,300), which was the wages for the organisation's workers. On their return, the lorry was ambushed just outside the city by heavily armed civilians who took the money and purchases and made off in a car without number plates. "We're sure it was the military who carried out the assault," says Gloria.

At present the Committee is busy with an education programme to teach people all over northern Morazán about their rights. They are thinking of trying to organise sessions on women's rights too. The other major activity is to prepare documentation for the Truth Commission and the Ad Hoc Commission on all the crimes committed by the army against the civilian population since 1980.

"We've already uncovered seven other massacres in addition to the well-known case of El Mozote: Villa el Rosario in October 1980; Junquillo in 1981 at almost the same time as Mozote; Caserío La Golondrina, Jocoaitique; El Tule, Gualococti, in the municipality of Osicala; Cerro Pando – which we knew of before, but now we've found new witnesses; and La Guacamaya, here in Meanguera, on 13 October 1980. There are others too: the hamlets of Agua Blanca, and Sunsulaca, both in Cacaopera.

Just the other week Toribio went with some volunteers to Corinto [south of the Torola] to gather testimonies. Over 200 people came forward. Because they were in the government controlled area, this was perhaps the first time they had dared to speak out. We recorded 112 separate testimonies which we're collating at the moment to present to the Truth Commission.

My own family comes from the hamlet of La Guacamaya, and relatives of mine were killed in the Mozote massacre. My cousin Rosa Lidia Pereira, was married to José Marcos Díaz, who owned a lorry and a shop in El Mozote. They had three children, Irma aged four, Lorena three, and Amilcar aged two months. All of them were killed in the massacre, together with José's father, stepmother and stepbrother."

9
The Land

The cow lies awkwardly in the ditch beside the road, legs pawing the air, bellowing piteously, her back broken. A crowd of spectators has gathered. The creature must have dragged her tether and fallen the hundred feet or so from the Quebrachos plateau above. Every available yard here is cultivated, and the maize plants nod their tresses right up to the edge of the cliff. Don Chepe had bought the cow only yesterday, and the loss is a serious blow to him. When we return in the afternoon, everything edible has been cut up and removed, and only a heap of steaming offal remains beside the road.

Few people in the Community can afford cows and those who can, usually have only one or two. Even if people could afford to buy more, there is almost no land to pasture a herd. Pigs are much cheaper and easier to feed, which explains why there is a pig rootling around almost every house. A few people have goats and nearly everyone has five or six chickens.

The scattered housing on the road between Quebrachos and San Luis is more like that of the traditional hamlet. Whereas in Quebrachos and San Luis there is a piped water supply, these people have to clamber down a steep gorge to a spring. But they have more space for their *parcela* or kitchen garden than other members of the Community. They are closer too to their own *milpa* where they grow the maize, beans and sorghum on which the family depends for its staple diet. Before the war, many families had *tierra*, a larger expanse of land, on which they would grow not only their subsistence crops but also some cash crops. At CSM, however, there is no spare land and what there is is mostly too poor and too precipitous to support cultivation of any cash crops except sisal. Where they have sufficient space and some protection from the trampling feet of neighbours, children, and untethered pigs, families devote a lot of effort to their *parcelas*, growing not only vegetables and fruit, but herbs and flowers. Up in Quebrachos, Rufina's garden has several big banana trees with squash vines rambling all over them like ivy; a fruiting beanstalk climbing up another tree on which she has hung the empty carapace of an armadillo she surprised and killed the other day. The armadillo, called *cusuco* in El Salvador, is good to eat when stewed with cabbage and yucca and lots of spices. Herbs and spices are grown in the garden too: there are several kinds of chili, one with glossy purple fruits like miniature aubergines, some spring onions growing in a terracotta pot, and pungent oregano with leaves two inches across, a far cry from our dainty marjoram.

Several houses near the road have huge woodpiles stacked up next to them and we see young boys dragging branches across the slopes to cut up for firewood. In theory, people in the Community are not supposed to cut live wood, but some of the branches look suspiciously green, and further up the slope we see the white scars of amputation on living trees. The hillsides are being denuded by the pressure of a close-packed community of 8,000, almost all of whom use firewood for cooking and clear every available inch of land for maize.

*****

To the right of the road the ground drops down a slope of at least one in five. A patch of earth a hundred yards by fifty has been cleared beside the road. A man is sowing: in his left hand he has a long stick with a bill-hook tied to the tip, with which he hollows out a little hole in the rich, loose humus; with his right he drops in a single seed at a time, and then dips again into a plastic can he has tied around his waist to carry the grain.

"What are you sowing?"

"Sorghum."

"What's the soil like?"

"Good. Look down there!" He points to some tall, lush maize plants growing further down.

"Do you think you'll get good yields for some years to come?"

"We'll have to see. We ought to let the soil lie fallow."

"Did you always sow your *milpa* in the same place in the old days?"

"No. One year in one place, and the next in another, to let the soil rest. We came back to the same plot every other year."

He picks up a handful of rich brown humus and crumbles it between his fingers. "This is the stuff that makes the maize grow; but when it rains hard all this gets washed down into the rivers."

"Is there enough land here for you to rotate the *milpa*?"

"That's the problem. There are a lot of people here and hardly any land."

*****

In the whole coastal region, in the east of the country,
All of us peasants grow maize.
Maize baking in the pan smells like a pretty girl,
And when it is in flower, even the stalks are sweet.
(from a song by Conjunto Morazán, CSM's musical group)

Milpa is fundamental. Almost every family in Ciudad Segundo Montes sows a *milpa* plot, and since the free distribution of food aid ceased in December 1991, the grain crop is vital for the family's subsistence. Each family finds and marks out their own plot. The lucky ones find land close to their house, but others may have to walk for up to an hour. We ask whether there are disputes about boundaries, and how they are resolved, but we are told that by and large they don't occur. There are no fences or hedges or marker stones: apparently people mark their territory by eye and by reference to trees and rocks. The terrain is so hilly and broken that level fields or even strips are an impossibility.

Milpa means maize but some people also plant sorghum and beans. Normally it is the man who works the *milpa*, but some women do so as well, especially in CSM, where over 70 per cent of the economically active population is female. A big USAID survey of agriculture in El Salvador in 1988 found that over one third of agricultural producers were women. Like many of the older women, and those with jobs in the Community, Rufina employs labourers to work her *milpa* for her. They are paid in kind, taking an agreed percentage of the harvest. Helena, who works in the cafeteria at Quebrachos, says:

"I know how to grow maize. Lots of women don't do it, but I always have, all my life. I'm very fond of working on the land. I like gardens, but most of all I like to grow maize. First of all you have to clear the land, then you sow the seed. We just make a little hole with the hoe. Then you put the maize in, three or four seeds to each hole. And in each hole you also place two beans."

In El Salvador, you get two maize crops a year. The first crop is sown in April or May and harvested in August. The second is sown in August and harvested in November/December. Sorghum is sown in January and sometimes a second crop in July. Beans, which grow quickly, are sown in among the maize plants and harvested earlier.

The *milpas* in Ciudad Segundo Montes are tiny, about three quarters of an acre on average, according to a study carried out in early 1992 by

IDEA, a Salvadorean research institute. There is not enough land for them to be larger, and in any case most households don't have enough able-bodied adults to work a larger plot. There is some unused land in the wider area surrounding the Community, but people are afraid to use it, as Juan Mejía, a Jesuit priest and agronomist, explains:

"Last year a man was gathering firewood not far from the Community when he stepped on a mine and was killed. People are frightened to go into areas which haven't been cleared of mines. ONUSAL is supposed to be removing them, but it will take time and cooperation from the former belligerents."

The *milpa* plot alone is clearly not enough, even for bare subsistence. According to Juan Bautista:

"An average family really needs 10 – 12 *manzanas* [17 – 21 acres] of land, but no one has as much as that here. A lot of us only have between one and two *manzanas* of *milpa*. I sow about one *manzana* [1.75 acres] at the moment: we get two harvests, so it lasts most of the year. But if we had 12 *manzanas*, we could give over one *manzana* each to coffee, sugar cane and sisal, which we could sell. The rest we could use for growing subsistence crops and cattle pasture... It's hard to live solely from the *milpa*. We'll have to see how we're going to survive."

It is a long time, though, since the average family in Morazán had anything like 12 *manzanas* of land. As Lencho the catechist says,

"Even before the war we only had small plots. Our grandparents had quite a lot of land, but our families are large and in no time at all we had nothing, because they divided the land to give each child a plot. So now the average plot is not enough for a family to live on. I knew one family who had nothing at all, just the land their house stood on. I wonder what happened to their children? They'd have to work as day labourers and go down to the coast at harvest time to cut cane."

In line with the thinking of the leadership, Juan José predicts that the importance of the *milpa* may diminish in due course:

"Perhaps in the long run, if the Community develops in a more urban way, the question of land will cease to be so important. It's true that when people came back here, the first thing they did was sow a *milpa*. That's no bad thing, and it's essential, though it's the worst and the

Father and son harvesting maize on the family's *milpa*   Jenny Matthews

hardest work there is. But the land just won't sustain people any more."

The agronomist Juan Mejía is not so sure:

"It's such a basic part of the culture. The various attempts at change and land reform have never got around this. The process of decentralisation and greater autonomy in CSM means that people will continue to cling to their individual family plots.

I don't think the solution is to discourage cultivation of family plots; we need to change how they cultivate them. Apart from maize, sorghum and beans, we want to encourage people to try more profitable and less ecologically harmful crops.

Families rely on *milpa* for their own consumption and for feeding their pigs and chickens. All they sell is the maize plants for fodder after the harvest. As the Community progresses, people may start to think of the *milpa* more as a source of income."

*****

Since the signing of the Peace Accords in January 1992, property rights have become a complex and potentially conflictive issue throughout El Salvador, and Ciudad Segundo Montes is no exception. When the Community was established, people just sowed their *milpa* on the nearest bit of free land, but as José, a Community teacher, explains:

"Now the situation is changing a bit. In the future we're going to have to talk to the people who own the land and get their agreement, rather than just working the nearest vacant plot as we do now."

Quite a number of the inhabitants of CSM owned land before the war which now lies within the confines of the Community. It would have been impossible even in peacetime to establish such a large new community in one place while respecting all the existing titles and boundaries. According to one international worker, while the refugees were still in Colomoncagua, some 387 of them were identified as owning land on the site for the repatriation. They were consulted and a deal was struck under which they agreed not to press any claim for their former land. Now, with title to land one of the most complex and conflicting aspects of the peace process, some of them are beginning to demand their land back.

Apparently one of the factors in the refugees' decision to repatriate in 1989 was their fear of losing legal title to their land if they failed to return within ten years. However, it is doubtful whether anyone had a clear strategy at that point. There was a large group of refugees to relocate and a vast area of almost empty, depopulated countryside in which to locate them. Juan José says:

"At first the FMLN's demand was that the government should simply legalise the lands, and that would be that. The land would be 'won' and it would be up to the government to pay the former owners. Later, during the peace negotiations, it was suggested that there should be an inventory of land the FMLN claimed for itself and its people, and that the government should respect the *de facto* tenure patterns existing in this zone [northern Morazán]. After six months the government would establish legal mechanisms to satisfy all parties – the present occupiers and the former owners. But the government has been making all sorts of excuses about the cost...

We proposed some time ago that the government expropriate all these lands [at CSM], and hand them over to us as communal property so that later we can devise a mechanism – which could take many years – whereby every person gets offered a plot. That would be much easier than the government allocating the individual titles. It seems the stumbling block is that the government wants us to pay for the land. First they drive us off our own land and make us into refugees, then they expect us to buy the land back.

The only solution is for the owners of the land, even those who are living in the Community now, to be paid compensation. We can't just give them back their land – it would be impossible. It's all divided up into little plots, with different people living on it and sowing their *milpa*. We certainly believe that everyone's property rights should be respected, and that the government should pay everyone who has to give up land. No one is going to be evicted from any piece of land."

*****

The Community's own Land Office is just below the Cultural Centre at San Luis. People are arriving to register claims to land that lies within the 5,000 acres that make up Ciudad Segundo Montes, based on their use or title before the war.

An elderly man called Narciso Argueta has come in to claim two plots, one in Hatos and one in Poza Honda. He is given one form to fill in for both. The Land Office will present the form to the land sub-commission of COPAZ, the Commission for the Consolidation of Peace, established in January 1992 and made up of representatives of the government, political parties and the FMLN.

The special difficulty for land within Ciudad Segundo Montes is that at the time of the repatriation it was allocated without regard for previous ownership, and much of it is occupied for communal use – by workshops, stores, schools, clinics, and the Community's own agricultural projects: the chicken farm, the cattle ranch, the tree nursery, etc. Apparently a joint committee of the government, the FMLN and ONUSAL has now agreed that the government will compensate former owners of land now occupied by any public building. Besides the negotiations between the FMLN and the government, CSM is attempting to raise funds from the international community to buy at least 2,600 acres.

The options for Narciso and other individual claimants are: to persuade the present occupier or CSM to vacate his land; to sell it to the Community; or to ask the government to intervene. The latter option is a poor one, as legal processes are likely to be slow and expensive and Narciso, unless he has powerful friends, might well lose. Eviction of the present occupier is prohibited under the terms of the Peace Accords. It has happened in other parts of the country (sometimes with violent consequences), but is most unlikely in northern Morazán. CSM leaders stress that as yet no conflict has arisen between the Community and individual members over land titles. Of the 291 claimants, 238 are willing to sell their property and 53 are refusing to do so. A family group come into the office, headed by a large and rather domineering man in a baseball cap. The landowner seems to be the woman in the group, though the men do most of the talking. She owns land somewhere around Cerro Pando, with three houses which are occupied, but not by members of her family. She is not from CSM and hasn't brought any documentation. Quite a lot of land in CSM is owned by people outside the Community, most of whom spent the war in the government controlled areas around San Francisco Gotera and San Miguel. There is considerable mutual suspicion and some open hostility between these people and the repatriated refugees, but the outsiders can do little in an area which is completely controlled by the Community and protected by the FMLN.

Narciso has a title to only one of his two plots, so under the COPAZ rules he will have to present four witnesses who are not relatives but own neighbouring plots of land or can testify that he lived where he says he did. Another old man in the office has come to claim for a house-plot, but says that his documents all got burnt. Documents, or rather the lack of them, are a major problem for people trying to establish title to land. Only 45 out of the 291 claimants to land in CSM have titles. Many title deeds were lost or burned during the war, and the destruction of town halls meant the loss of the birth registers. Despite promises made by the government before they repatriated, most CSM members still have no proper identity papers. All of this means that any legal process will be slow, expensive and risky, and for the most part people have a considerable interest in reaching agreement by negotiation.

*****

José Emilio Medina Lobos is one of a group of 254 FMLN war-wounded who recently arrived home from Cuba, where they had been sent for intensive medical care, rehabilitation and occupational therapy under the Castro Government's solidarity programme. They were welcomed home at a tumultuous rally organised by the FMLN in San Salvador and then divided up among the many communities that had offered to provide them with homes. Ciudad Segundo Montes took 52 of them — a generous gesture considering the serious disabilities of many of the war-wounded.

José Emilio works as the administrator in the CSM brickworks. Like all the war-wounded on both sides, he is entitled to a plot of land under the terms of the Peace Accords. But it is highly unlikely that the land will be in Morazán.

"There's a possibility they will give us better land, in Usulután. They're going to distribute plots on the California estate, near Jiquilisco. We're not sure whether we'll stay here or go there. We're happy here. I was given work within two months of arriving... We think that the sacrifices we made in the course of this war give us the right to get something under the Accords. If we do get land, it doesn't necessarily mean leaving here. I think we should go down and take possession of the land, but come back here again afterwards: at least we'll have the land."

Not only the war-wounded but all the demobilised FMLN fighters are supposed to receive a grant of land, notionally about four *manzanas* [seven acres], under the terms of the Peace Accords. Since CSM is down to accommodate up to 800 demobilised fighters, some of whom are already here, and many of whom have relatives living in the Community, the effects of this land grant, if it ever materialises, will be profound. If the beneficiaries decide to move to their land, then many will take at least some members of their family with them, and there will be a substantial emigration from CSM. If they do not move, but rent out the land, or find family or friends to farm it for them, then potentially it could generate a small cash income for a large section of the CSM population. If, as is rumoured, the land is on the coastal plain in Usulután, then it will be many times more productive than the sparse soils of Morazán.

10
The Assembly

A score of smart new mountain bikes glint in the sunshine, leaning against the Teachers' Centre or propped on their kick-stands. Sturdy, brightly painted in red, pink or blue, with modern indexed gearing, they look strangely incongruous in Morazán. Yet where better? This is ideal territory for a mountain bike – not city streets, but real mountains: precipitous slopes, boulders, and deep mud in the rainy season.

The bikes are the brainchild of Rudi, a German volunteer who has been working with the Community since Colomoncagua days. He obtained them for some of the teachers in the Community's primary schools. It's a two-hour walk down from Jocoaitque and a good hour from El Barrial. The bikes save valuable time and help to improve attendance at the afternoon training sessions. Along with their uniforms, they also confer a certain status on the teachers.

"We started out with ten bicycles, three for women, seven for men. The women were very upset at first, because men made remarks – they'd never seen a woman on a bicycle before. There was no tradition of using bikes in the countryside here: people went everywhere on foot."

Rudi raises funds through friends in Germany. The bicycles are bought from an ecological cooperative in San Salvador which assembles them from imported parts, and gives employment to people injured in the war. They cost around 1,600¢ (£115) each, slightly more for the women's model. The bicycles are not given away but sold for about a third of the real cost, and the teachers pay in monthly quotas of 50¢ (£3.60), about 15% of their monthly wage. They're not allowed to resell them for three years. The money raised goes to finance more bicycles. The project has been a huge success. Fifty-two bicycles have been distributed so far, including two for the priests, and there's a waiting list for 65 more within the Community.

*****

The Teachers' Centre is a small wooden building divided into two classrooms, with a wide verandah. The end-wall is completely covered by a brightly coloured mural depicting teachers and their classes in the open air, with the figure of Fr Segundo Montes looking on. Today is Saturday but the teachers have all turned up for a day-long assembly to discuss Target 2000, the document issued by the Community leaders, which is now being circulated amongst each of the Community's work-areas.

There are twelve discussion groups of about a dozen people each, some squashed into opposite corners of the classrooms, others on the verandah or under shadow of the eaves behind the building. The teachers are neatly dressed, many in their new uniform (in CSM it is the teachers, not the children, who wear uniform): for the women a check skirt and a white blouse with a light pink check pattern on collars and cuffs; for the men dark grey trousers, white shirt and black shoes. There is a complete cross-section of ages, from late teens to over sixty. Women are in the majority, especially in the middle age groups.

Each group has a paper listing various questions for discussion:
– We are always being told we are 'an island'. What do you think?
– Concerning the leadership and administration of the Community's structures:
List the three most positive aspects.
List the three most negative aspects.
List three actions we should undertake to improve the way the structures are run.
– What is your view on wages in the Community? Should they remain fixed or should they increase? Who should decide? The workers in each structure? Or the Community as a whole?
– What do you think about individual initiatives? Should they be encouraged or restricted?
– What effect will the demobilisation of the FMLN have?
– What are the five biggest obstacles which prevent the Community from advancing? What are our five greatest challenges?
– Are we making progress?
The method of discussion owes much to the catechesis groups, promoted by progressive priests during the 1970s and still practised by the base Christian communities today. Each group has a discussion leader and some of the leaders have a tough time trying to persuade the members to participate. Asked for their opinion, the teachers, especially the younger ones, tend to look at the floor, twist their hands in evident discomfort and

struggle over a few words. Some are lively, though, especially the older women. At the end of the allocated time, they break for lunch and then resume in plenary, as many as can fit crammed into the classroom, others spilling onto the verandah outside, to hear the report-backs from the groups. There is a crude p.a. system, which crackles and buzzes, distorting the voices of the rapporteurs. Each group in turn is asked for its report. Most have written out their answers and reply succinctly to each of the questions in the discussion paper, identifying the topic, or asking the chair of the plenary to read out first the text of each question they discussed. The report-backs are clear and articulate. Five out of the twelve groups have women rapporteurs, and the chair of the plenary is a woman.

There is a high degree of unanimity among the groups. Peace is good but has brought problems: there has been an increase in crime, especially robbery, and social problems such as drinking; and there are serious difficulties over land, with former owners wanting to reclaim their property. If CSM is isolated, it is because the government has refused to recognise it, has delayed giving documents to the repatriates, provides little or no aid for Northern Morazán, and doesn't recognise the work of the Community, its teachers, and the educational qualifications of the children. The way to change the situation is to press for legalisation, documentation and government support for the work of the Community.

On the Community's leadership, several of the groups are openly critical. They complain of the lack of information and consultation. Aid money is poorly allocated with some organisations getting the lion's share of money and vehicles. The teachers claim they're not told what happens to the funding. There's a lack of trained administrators and technicians and too much centralisation. Group 5 says, for instance:

"The expenditure on infrastructure here in the Community is very high. It's worrying to hear talk of repopulating old hamlets elsewhere like Guacamaya and Poza Honda. What's the point of doing all this here, if everyone is going to go back to their old homes? Funds are not being spent on clinics, hospitals and schools; the people working in administration should modify their attitudes or take courses in human relations – particularly the central administration, because we sometimes get short shrift from them. We want the leadership to change its mentality and stop showing preference for its members' friends and relatives; in the name of the Community, we ask that the funds, and the materials which are sold, be used for the welfare of the Community, for the elders, for orphan children, for people who are unable to work, although we see that none of this is included in the agenda of this discussion; another negative thing is the waste of feed in the cattle project, the CODECO store, etc. They seem to prefer seeing things going off to lowering the price or giving them away to those who need them."

Everyone agrees that wages in the Community should be increased. Most think that the levels should be fixed by the workers in each sector, in consultation with the Community leadership. Surprisingly for a service sector such as education, four groups argue for performance-related pay: people should be paid 'according to the work they do'; 'you can't raise the wages of someone who just turns up but doesn't do the work'; pay should be related to 'the knowledge, efficiency and productivity of each worker'. Everyone agrees that 'individual initiatives' such as tiny front-room shops in people's houses, individual craft trades like tailoring should be supported, so long as they don't adversely affect the Community. They should be given credit from the Bank, and helped to form cooperatives. One group argued that such enterprises should pay a monthly quota to support the Community's social services.

The return of the mayor to the Meanguera municipality and the reconstruction of the municipal offices is supported, though some groups argue that the new municipal centre should be in Ciudad Segundo Montes rather than Meanguera. This would improve the legal status of the Community in the eyes of national government, make it easier to negotiate for government grants and projects, and help individuals to obtain documentation. But it should be a new kind of municipal council, 'not like in the old days': it should be committed to protecting CSM and its leaders should be elected by the Community.

The teachers believe that demobilised fighters from the FMLN should be resettled in the Community, but they are clearly apprehensive about the effects, and not afraid to say so. Group 5 decided, "the likely effects would be: more antisocial behaviour; more unemployment; more children. We can support them by creating more jobs and giving them educational talks about antisocial behaviour and family planning. If we do nothing, we may confront corruption, bad manners, social decomposition, and robberies. They should be given loans at low interest."

Plans to repopulate the nearby areas of Guacamaya and Poza Honda (less than an hour's walk from CSM) are supported, but first roads must be built and the means found to provide water supplies, houses, and health and education services.

The greatest challenges facing the Community are seen as the problem of defining and legalising land tenure; providing more employment; maintaining and improving the Community's infrastructure and social services; and obtaining decent housing for every family. The greatest obstacles to development are the lack of technical, administrative and commercial skills (every group mentions this); the lack of legal documents, land titles and legal status for the Community and its various projects and services; and the scarcity of land and jobs.

After the last group has reported back, there is a summing-up by Isaias who is in charge of education for the whole Community. A small, slightly wizened figure in his late fifties, he peers sternly at his audience over horn-rimmed spectacles:

"All the groups have had a very good discussion and done what we asked for... We are discussing the strategy we want to follow until the year 2000. You know what our lives were like in the refugee camp: a society which lived on charity, in a democratic situation where everyone was equal... When we arrived back here, we set up the structures and organisations, and that was a big difference from the past. Now we see that these organisations are working in a way which has to be changed... We have to find a better way, and in particular we have to decentralise. It's up to us, the Community's workers, to do it. That's what we have been discussing today... All your opinions will be taken into account. We will take them to the next General Assembly."

The teachers stand chatting for a while and then drift off homewards. It has been an impressive meeting, though not everyone is satisfied. As one of the education advisers grumbles, they have been pressing for some time for an assembly to discuss the problems of education. "What we got, though, was the Target 2000 discussion ordered by the Community leaders. It's a hierarchy here: they order something and everyone has to jump to it. This kind of general strategy debate isn't a good way of involving people: it's too high-level."

11

The People of El Barrial

The smallest of CSM's five settlements, El Barrial, stands like a sentinel on high ground, nearly three miles to the east of its sister settlements, at the end of a steep, treacherous unpaved road. A few of the Community's four-wheel-drive vehicles go there on specific errands but there is no public transport. The most dependable way of getting to El Barrial is on foot.

The two-hour walk takes us first through Los Hatos, past the poultry farms – long, low barns echoing with clucking and rustling and planted round with hot orange zinnias – and the tree nursery, and over the La Joya river, smaller and less muddy than the Torola, where women are slapping wet clothes vigorously on big, smooth boulders on the riverbanks. Then it is just a steady climb through *milpa* and grassland, sparsely scattered with scrub and a few tall trees. But the settlement, when we reach it, is surprisingly rich in mature trees, survivors of bombs and fires: fruit trees such as mango, avocado and orange, and giant guanacastes on whose ribbed roots people sit to talk and relax.

El Barrial was the site of savage massacres, says Don José María, whom we meet husking his crop of red beans outside his house. "Right where we're standing there was a big massacre, lots of people were killed. The massacre of Cerro Pando happened just up there" – pointing to a near-vertical mountainside overhanging the village and planted with maize in apparent defiance of gravity – "and over there, La Guacamaya, La Joya." It is said that when the people returned to El Barrial, they found all its wells choked with human remains.

These days, water is brought up to the settlement from springs near El Mozote, over four miles away. The abundant shade and water and the villagey atmosphere make El Barrial an agreeable place to live. But it is a very obvious outpost from the rest of the community. Was there any element of strategy in its siting? According to Salustino Barrera, the head of the office of Urban Development, which was responsible for the siting and topographical planning of CSM, the determining factors were the pleasant climate and space for pasture and vegetable and fruit growing.

*****

El Barrial is unique among the CSM settlements in having a central green space. From a distance it looks not unlike an English village green: broad, treeless and tranquil. The laughter of women and the happy shrieks of splashing children float across the green from the communal standpipe in the centre of it.

Ranged along the sides of this green are several wooden buildings. One of these is the children's day-nursery. Inside, it is hot, close, dark. Half a dozen women are sitting, each with a child in her lap, while other children tumble aimlessly about the floor or stand at the door looking out onto the sunstruck green. There are very few toys. A huge-eyed toddler swings dreamily on the slatted gate that divides this room from the quiet end of the nursery where the babies sway gently in hammocks like silkworms in their cocoons. Here, one or two young women are feeding their babies at the breast. Nothing else is happening. Each of CSM's settlements has a nursery, and this one is poorly resourced and half-heartedly run compared with most of the others; but it is particularly necessary, because El Barrial itself provides few work opportunities apart from the school, the clinic, and the nursery itself, and most people here who have jobs with the Community go down to San Luis to work.

*****

At this time of day, it is mostly older people who are to be found at home. Rafaela, thin as a rail, greets us from her front door. She is a potter and shows us some of her rounded water-jars and big flat plates for cooking tortillas. She learned her craft well before the war and practised it in Colomoncagua, but has no work with the Community now because, she says, she is too old. "And also, you know, the clay's just not the same here, it's too sandy; over in Torola it was a lot better."

Rafaela has three pieces of land, one in Torola and two in Santa Anita de Jocoaitique. She tells us she would like to claim them but feels it would be too difficult to return to them on her own. Widowed when her husband was killed by soldiers in 1980, she lives alone, though her son and three daughters all live in the Community. She doesn't like having to depend on the Community for the daily ration of tortillas provided by the Social Welfare department. She remembers how in Torola, there used to be feast-days and markets when she could sell her wares. She seems wistful, nostalgic for a kind of rural life that may be gone for ever.

More optimistic is Leonardo Portillo, who runs the library here, a small timber house with a deep veranda, lined inside with bookshelves holding

The library, El Barrial   Jenny Matthews

a motley collection of books: some children's books, elementary maths
and geography textbooks, single copies of classics like Don Quixote
obviously donated by passing visitors, and dozens of Spanish grammars.
Don Leonardo is one of the very few people in CSM who was able to
return from Honduras to his original plot of land and find his house
relatively undamaged.

*****

Vicenta, who works in the nursery, insists on giving us lunch: golden-
brown slices of fried plantain and a big cup of maize coffee. While we
are eating it, a good-looking young man in olive-green trousers emerges
from the house. He's passing through on his way down from the FMLN
military base near Perquín, for he is an ex-combatant still 'pending
demobilisation', as he puts it. "Are you Doña Vicenta's son?" we ask.
   "Adopted son," he replies. All his family were killed in the massacre
at El Tule, near Torola, where Doña Vicenta and her family also lived;
Vicenta took him and two other children orphaned in the massacre to
Colomoncagua, together with her own seven children. He was six when

they fled to Colomoncagua in 1980; years later he returned to El Salvador, joined the FMLN, and fought for two and a half years. Like so many young Salvadoreans, he must have joined up at fourteen or fifteen.

"Have you ever been back to where you lived?"

"No, and I probably wouldn't recognise it if I did, I was so young when we left. Besides, what's there any more?"

Perhaps because of his youth, Vicenta's adopted son is more unequivocal than most about this issue. On the whole, it is the older people who nurse the dream of returning one day to their home villages. El Barrial has lost more people than the other settlements through 'emigration' not only to places of origin but also to more distant repopulations like Lempa Mar in Usulután by the coast. There are now only 972 people here. Anastasio Caballero, the last person we visit today, says two things are largely to blame: El Barrial's relative isolation and the lack of any public transport linking it to San Luis or Los Hatos, and the failure of any permanent housing to materialise so far. "You see movement, activity, houses being built in the other settlements, but not here," he says. "They marked out lots, but they didn't get any further."

Tacho, as he is known, and his wife Arminda have no intention of leaving El Barrial, although life here is hardly cushy for them. Tacho is 62 now and has no waged work with the community. They are both very active in pastoral work, but the work is unpaid: "It only takes a few hours a week, we just go to meetings; but there's always our work in the *milpa* to keep us going."

"What about your tailoring?" Tacho is sitting at an aged treadle-operated Singer as we talk, making a pair of grey trousers.

He pushes his glasses up onto his forehead. "It doesn't bring in much. I sew mostly for the family. I learned it in Colomoncagua, I was in the tailoring workshop there. In the refuge Arminda worked in the collective kitchens and the nursery but she hasn't worked outside the house since coming back. Mind you, there's only us two and our granddaughter, and we don't spend much!"

In contrast, Arminda's sister Adela and her husband, who are also visiting this afternoon, have already begun the process of reclaiming the family land in Volcancillo, near Jocoaitique, and are keen to return there. They went south in 1980 and spent the war years, first in a camp for the displaced, then in a more permanent 'suburb' on the outskirts of San Francisco Gotera. Urban life has given them opportunities unavailable to their relatives in Honduras: their eldest daughter is just finishing her first year at university. "But I hate the town," says Adela, gazing with satisfaction at Arminda's chili bushes and orange trees and the panorama of mountains and cornfields beyond. "It's noisy, there's traffic, it's hot, the air's bad, and everything costs money. You know, we even have to pay for firewood and water!"

*****

The afternoon is drawing to a close. We reach El Barrial's grocery store just in time to grab a warm soft drink before it shuts at 4pm. Zoila, the young single mother who runs it, reveals another of the difficulties of isolation: in the wet, even four-wheel-drive vehicles can't always get up here, so fresh food is a problem: she either has to buy large consignments and risk the food deteriorating before it can be sold, or smaller quantities which may then run out. This is El Barrial's only community-run shop; there are one or two others, Zoila says, but they are much smaller, little more than a crate of Cokes and a few bags of crisps sold from someone's house.

As we descend, we are greeted by people on their way home from work. A group of young teachers are proudly wheeling their new bicycles over the rockier stretches of road; Fermín, another of Vicenta's sons, who works in the photography and video workshop of the Social Communication department, is bringing up a small camera to take some pictures of the clinic; Jaime, in charge of Communal Services for El Barrial, bent double and plodding, smiles out from under the huge sack of maize on his shoulders. The evening is cool, the air clear and scented; from the river at Los Hatos, where you can swim, the laughter of children is carried up on the breeze.

12
Khaki and Curd Cheese

One of the largest and most solidly-constructed buildings in Ciudad Segundo Montes houses the clothing and shoemaking workshops, generally known as 'the clothing factory'. Set back from the main road just below the power station, it certainly looks more like a small factory than the other workshops.

Felicita, the administrator, greets us from her desk in a large entrance area which doubles as a kind of showroom (although there is no sign outside or on the road to indicate you can buy things here). The only other things in the room are a rope stretched between big nails on which sample garments are hanging, and some large bolts of cloth. Through the open doorway come the sound of hammering, the whirr of industrial sewing machines, snatches of music from a radio. Felicita takes us through. Widely spaced in a long, echoing room are twenty industrial sewing machines interspersed with cutting tables. At the far end, a smaller number of larger stitching and soling machines comprise the shoemaking workshop which shares the space with the garment workshop. The floor is strewn with leather and rubber offcuts and piles of half-finished black army-style boots. There are fluorescent lights and plenty of power-points for the machines, only about half of which are in use. Felicita tells us:

"Twenty-five of us work here. We haven't been able to expand as we should, because we haven't been getting the regular orders we need. We had serious problems at the beginning and accumulated big stocks which didn't sell. Recently we've improved sales of what we're making now, but not of the old stock."

Quite a lot of the 'old stock' is on display, folded in neat piles: shirts and blouses, frilly aprons and little girls' dresses, T-shirts, nearly all in a narrow range of plain pastel colours, very dull in comparison with the cheap but bright-coloured garments and jeans the traders bring up from Gotera every day. It seems no surprise that they don't sell: these garments are exactly like those the refugees produced in Colomoncagua. Felicita says they are learning from their mistakes:

"At first we produced haphazardly, without thinking about fashion or people's preferences. Also, the cloth we were using wasn't of very good quality. We brought a lot of the cloth with us from Honduras, but recently we've started buying here. We still use some of the old cloth, but incorporate it into new designs."

There were other problems with using the cloth left over from Honduras. People resented having to pay for clothes identical to those they received free in Colomoncagua and made of cloth they knew was donated. Also, says Felicita, while the war was still in progress,

"some people were afraid to buy our clothes, because they were different, and made them easily identifiable to the authorities, especially if they went somewhere outside the zone, like Gotera."

The best use of the cloth from Honduras is to sell it by the yard to people from outside the Community, to whom it is new.

The factory has had one substantial order from the END, the FMLN army, for 50 olive-green shirts and trousers, and it made civilian clothes for some FMLN leaders when they first started going to San Salvador or abroad for meetings and negotiations. The latter were provided at ¢145 (just over £10) for an outfit of shirt and trousers, relatively fashionably cut. The END, incidentally, have also given the shoemaking workshop its only large order to date, for 2,000 pairs of boots – ironically, an order so large that the workshop is having trouble meeting the deadline with the current staff.

We ask about pricing.

"It depends on the cloth. We've got trousers at ¢70 (£5) the pair, some at ¢65, and some made from the cloth we brought from Honduras at ¢35 ... Now we've changed the styles people are buying more. But as most people in the community have very little money, they have to buy things as cheaply as possible ...

A lot of the clothes people buy in El Salvador are imported from Guatemala and from the US, and perhaps from Mexico. But this country also produces a lot of cheap garments. We're trying to compete, and especially to produce better quality goods. It's difficult to compete on price, because we pay high prices for our raw materials. We've started to work in assembly lines so we can produce more cheaply."

Do the clothes sell outside the Community?

"We only started selling outside the Community earlier this year, after the Peace Accords ... We've taken samples and some stock and sold to people in Gotera and San Miguel, and lately we've had buyers come from San Salvador and take quite large quantities from us, both of the old stock and of our newer products.

We have two salespeople but they have to cover all the workshops in the Community; they don't just work on clothing. They travel around with samples of hammocks, sheetmetal, from the craft workshops, shoes, everything."

But in spite of this interest from outside the Community, the fact is that the factory, far from expanding, has been slimming down. Earlier in the year it sold off some sewing machines which are now being used privately – creating yet more competition for the clothing factory. What are its prospects?

Like all the workshops, the factory urgently needs technical assistance – in design, quality control, and especially marketing. Its staff are only just beginning to recognise the need to produce for a potential market, rather than simply responding to a tightly specified order such as the one from the END. They could also collaborate profitably with other entities within the Community itself. For instance, the factory has big stocks of plain white or pastel-coloured T-shirts. The Community also has facilities for printing, but the screen-printing workshop, part of Social Communication, buys in T-shirts to print from outside. It hasn't occurred to anyone that the two workshops might work together for mutual benefit, generating income for both.

*****

Management of all the Community's productive activities is currently centralised in CODEMO. The organisation was set up at the time of repatriation as the Emergency Committee for Morazán when the newly returned refugees needed a structure to organise emergency supplies. It has been renamed the Development Committee for Morazán.

Blanca, the administrator, gives us strong coffee in small china cups and tells us about CODEMO's current remit. There are four divisions, she says, each with a coordinator and a number of subordinate areas: the semi-industrial workshops – clothing and footwear, forged and sheet metal, the garage, and the brickworks; the handicraft workshops – pottery, sisal products, and leatherwork; livestock – cattle, pigs, chickens, goats, and rabbits; and agriculture – basic grains, fruit and vegetables. Almost immediately, however, she qualifies this by saying that some of these are being reduced. The small rabbit- and goat-rearing projects are shortlisted for handing over to the workers, as is the garage, and have already moved

Sale of eggs from the Community's chicken farm   Jenny Matthews

out from Los Hatos to Meanguera village. Vegetable production has been particularly problematic:

"We've been growing cucumber, chili, tomatoes, a little cabbage, but we've found that we haven't been able to control certain pests and the land isn't very good. Even though it's been lying fallow, we still haven't been able to get a much out of it."

By the time we leave the Community, the vegetable project has been closed down altogether, on the grounds that the expense of the necessary inputs is not justified by the yields. In fact, people here seem to regard vegetable growing as a domestic rather than a communal activity: many would like more space for their kitchen gardens and the new housing has been criticised for not allowing for them. Seventy per cent of the people interviewed in the IDEA study favoured the idea of diversifying family kitchen gardens so that people could cultivate for their own use and for sale.

So far no project has actually been handed over to its workers, but in our meetings with people in the Community we have found that everyone expects a wave of privatisation, without a very clear idea of what it involves. If an enterprise is handed over to the workers, we ask, will it belong to them? Will they have sole decision-making power? Will the income from the project belong to them or to the Community, or both? Do they have to contribute part of their earnings to the Community?

It all depends on the agreement between CODEMO and the workers at the outset, Blanca replies.

"For instance, the goat-rearing project has prospects for a good yield and represents a small investment. So we'll just transfer it to a few people... We're not expecting any further revenue for the Community in this case, but at least there'll be an income for those four families."

Once production improves, the families will have to start paying back the value of the Community's investment.

Blanca points out that larger and more potentially profitable enterprises, if privatised, would be expected to contribute to the Community out of their profits. If the chicken farm were to be privatised, for instance,

"the agreement would be different: they'd have to give some of the profit to the Community, and to areas like education and health which aren't productive but have to be financed....We don't want to let all that go."

In fact, it is very unlikely that the chicken farm will be privatised, at least in the short term. The Community is not thinking of privatising all productive projects, especially those with high levels of investment, few workers and the best prospects of generating resources for reinvestment or for financing social services. As the major owner of productive assets in the Community, CODEMO is understand-ably cautious about handing them over with no guarantee of recompense.

*****

After lunch we go with Darío to see the Community's cattle project. It is located in La Joya, possibly the most beautiful part of CSM, but almost unpopulated because of extensive war devastation. A bumpy twenty-minute drive from San Luis brings us out in a sheltered valley through which the little La Joya river runs chuckling along under trees. Here, fruit groves – pineapples, bananas, pawpaw, and coconut – are being planted. We pass the piggery, which began operating with twelve brood sows and two boars only in March. Both the piggery and the cattle project are cofinanced by the European Community and various European development agencies. Both projects depend heavily on aid, particularly to install the infrastructure necessary for modern livestock farming.

This is considerable: the cattle project has byres and concrete-floored pens, including a milking shed and a 'nursery' for newborn calves, oblong brick and cement water troughs, a big water tank, and a shed housing the feed mixer, a wicked-looking machine for shredding leaves and green branches, running off a small petrol engine and operated by two boys. Then there is the creamery, and a site office. Here we meet Claros, who is in charge of the project, and Amparo, who works in the creamery.

The herd currently numbers 85. The patriarch is a bull called 'Tyson', presumably because of his size – and his amorous proclivities. However, he is getting so heavy he will soon be unusable, as his weight could break the legs of the cows he mounts. By the end of the year he could be beef stew, and two younger replacements have already been bought.

Various dairy products are being produced – milk, *cuajada* (a kind of curd cheese), hard white cheese and cream. Amparo invites us to try the fresh batch of cheese in the creamery. Inside the cool brick building are wooden tables, cheese-presses and forms. Outside, metal vats, buckets, bowls and ladles, and plastic jerrycans and urns are drying on a long trestle in the sun. Muslin cloths for wrapping and straining cheese hang on a line. Salvadorean cheese is white, friable and salty, rather like Greek fetta.

Amparo cuts us slivers to taste from an eighteen-inch cubical block. It is delicious, rich-textured and sweet, far better than any cheese we've had in the cafeterias, or in restaurants in San Salvador for that matter. What's the secret?

"It's got cream in it," Amparo says. "Most cheese is made with skimmed milk, but we leave some of the cream in, so it's not so dry and crumbly. Also, we don't use so much salt." The cheese costs ¢12 a pound, about half the usual price. We ask where it's being sold. "Well, we're not really selling it outside the Community yet," Amparo says. "We've got to get production up. This is just the beginning." In fact, consumption so far is limited to a few community organisations.

*****

"Ciudad Segundo Montes isn't self-sufficient in basic grains", says agronomist Juan Mejía, "and it never will be. There are 8,000 people here, and the Community's own production of maize and beans can't meet the demand. The Community will need to trade in order to buy maize and so it's important to marry agriculture and livestock with semi-industrial production, in which CSM is well placed to establish a market niche. We also need to concentrate on products with some degree of processing and a higher added value, such as cheese rather than milk and chicken-feed concentrate as well as eggs."

However, manufacturing production is the area in which the Community has most noticeably begun to develop trading links outside the Community. What about the big agricultural projects? Do they have good potential for making a profit in the future?

"Three of them do," Juan says; "the poultry project, which is intensive, and the semi-intensive pig and cattle projects. Meanguera is definitely not a good agricultural area but it's got potential for grazing cattle."

Pigs span the CSM economy, from the big, intensive community-level project to the family unit. Every family has one or two pigs; people started buying piglets soon after the return, and there is quite a brisk trade in them both within the Community and at the livestock market held at Osicala each Friday. "They really are piggy-banks!" says Juan. "Every family's last resort when things go wrong."

They have also been looking at ways to improve the breeding of these domestic pigs in conjunction with the intensive pig project. Apart from its practical benefits, this also seems a good way of using a community-level project to generate visible support for individual livelihoods in the

Community, countering criticisms that the benefits of community projects do not go beyond those who are directly involved with them.

But is there a middle way between the large community-wide project and the individual effort?

"We haven't ruled out such projects," Juan replies, "but we haven't promoted them either, maybe because of the urgency of the larger projects. I think we need to discuss how much we want to prioritise projects run by individual families and small collectives."

Juan is optimistic about the future of the projects but he thinks decentralisation is the way forward, the qualitative leap people will have to take if they are to control their own lives at last:

"We want to get people to take a greater part in the economic dynamics of the process. This is essential. It'll help to solve other problems if families have more scope to use their own initiative, if they feel that the projects are really their own, and if they can earn more for themselves. Decentralisation should solve the problem of economic passivity you can see in the Community today ... We think that yes, the projects will grow and employ more labour, but that with the decentralisation, the investment in each project should be repaid to the local government of the Community to undertake more projects."

*****

The manna of foreign aid to reduce investment costs and the social benefit to be derived from any productive activity, are key elements in all discussions about production in the Community. Ciudad Segundo Montes is still extremely aid-dependent: although some work areas have stopped subsidising wages, they're only able to pay their own wage bills because there is still an accumulated cushion of aid money. The Community must clearly engage with the market if it is to reincorporate itself into the local and national economy. Yet its relationship with capitalism is un-comfortable. No one wants to return to the past; as Darío says:

"to rest our hopes of development and a better standard of living on agriculture is to condemn ourselves to the past, to return to a role of complementing the agroexport model that's always been here and that was the cause of injustice in the first place. We have to come up with something different, if we're going to overcome marginalisation."

But the Community is sharply aware of the contradiction between private enterprise and Community values. Target 2000 recognises this:

"[The introduction of] small and micro-enterprise in order to stimulate the entrepreneurial spirit among individuals will doubtless appear totally contrary to our communitarian aspirations, but only by developing this model will we be able to generate the jobs we need, which currently don't exist ..."

The Community wants to be able to provide services to protect its vulnerable sectors, but a system has yet to be devised to ensure that profit-making productive and commercial activities, both public and private, contribute to the services.

Juan José, setting the issue in the wider context of CSM's integration into national life, sees taxation as the obvious mechanism:

"I think that once we have a municipal government, perhaps one of its priorities will be to install a taxation system which could meet precisely this need [of providing community services]. At present such a system doesn't exist; the only taxes we pay are those imposed by central government, the VAT for example. But once a local government is installed, there's a series of taxes which it could feasibly impose and which could be used to solve these problems."

These measures depend on another issue, the legal recognition of the Community, which also implies the return of national health and education services. Questions of ownership of the buildings used for productive purposes, and the land they stand on, have been shelved for the moment until the land issue is clarified nationally, but lurk in the wings as potential problems. In fact, the whole process is still very fluid and undefined, with every decision opening fresh issues to be resolved. On what basis will decentralised enterprises pay the Community for capital equipment? What if they default? What are the safety nets for them? How will cooperatives or associations of workers be organised? Will they have political representation within comumnity structures? Will their employment practices and wage policies be regulated? What percentage of their earnings or profits will be earmarked, and for which social projects?

Finally we ask, would the Community allow a capitalist company, a timber company, say, to come and set up within CSM?

"No," says Juan, "not at present. It's been tried, and CSM hasn't allowed it. They just don't want to repeat the worker/boss situation. It would be different if a company proposed a joint-capital venture. I think there have been proposals along those lines."

13
Government

In November 1990, Ciudad Segundo Montes held an ambitious international conference. Despite the disruptive effects of a large military operation in the zone at exactly the same time. The Community called the conference 'A Year of Experiences' and used it to report to funders and solidarity supporters, to evaluate for themselves the successes and failures of their first year back in El Salvador, and to make public their plans for the next two years.

In that scant year the Community had made formidable advances in resettling in Morazán and adapting to 'the new reality'. By the time the conference took place, 550 wooden houses, the San Luis clinic, the Cultural Centre and the dormitory at Quebrachos, and various other public buildings had been constructed; water services had been installed, the power station had been built and was supplying San Luis; new structures had been set up, such as the Bank, Urban Development, two liaison offices in San Salvador and one in Gotera; goats and rabbits were being farmed, and the Community had 5,000 hens producing on average 129,000 eggs a month; there were day nurseries, a community transport service, community radio and a musical group; four of the Colomoncagua workshops had been restarted and each family had claimed a plot of land and was cultivating its *milpa*. Until local production could be established, essential food aid was still being distributed.

*****

All this was only possible, especially in the context of war, by maintaining the quasi-military discipline that had underpinned the extraordinary unity and organisation of Colomoncagua. New local government structures were developed, with an elected communal committee for each settlement and sectoral organisations of women, elderly people, youth, children and men. A Representative Assembly of 38 representatives was elected on 1 May 1990, but the unelected *Junta Directiva* who had led the Community in the refugee camp remained in office 'provisionally'.

The 1990 report recognises both the virtues and the failings of a system in which:

'centralism and verticalism predominated. This generated solid organisation, unity, and homogeneity, with a generally politically aware community, and was extremely efficient as a response to communal problems: organisation was dense, discipline high – things which were very necessary as a strategy for survival against external threats.

On the other hand, centralism and verticalism created a bureaucratic apparatus that depended very heavily on central coordination and gave rise to a lack of initiative among people at all levels.'

The Community now proposed to establish a system of self-government based on participatory democracy, defined as 'the incorporation of all members of the Community into decision-making'.

Two years later, the most recent policy document, Target 2000, is tussling with the practicalities of a community that has become very diverse, no longer needs the iron discipline demanded by wartime, and must look towards becoming part of the country's ordinary local government structures:

'With the arrival of new people in CSM, its composition is becoming more heterogeneous, resulting in a diversity of social groups just as in the rest of society. We can see that the pattern of a unitary structure and an ideologically homogeneous population is in the process of breaking up.'

Target 2000 again proposes 'a complete break with the centralised, vertical concept we have had of CSM'. Attempts to make such a break have already been made, most notably at the July 1991 General Assembly when the provisional *Junta Directiva* which had led the Community since repatriation was replaced by an elected leadership (although the people on it are very largely the same people as before). The Assembly also debated 'opening up the economic model' – encouraging private income-generation – while at the same time uncoupling the Community's social and government structures from its productive structures: as Juan José explains,

"We proposed creating a government of Segundo Montes ... Its social division would consist of what is now Communal Services, Urban Development, Health, and Education."

A kind of constitution or 'Statutes for Living in Community' was proposed. But "increasingly the problem is how to earn our living; and we're embarking on a period so critical that practically all our energies are going into looking for ways to survive." This urgency has meant that economic decentralisation and privatisation have advanced much faster than the development of democratic structures in the Community; and many people question the extent to which centralism and verticalism really have been overcome. They feel that the gap between the leaders and the grassroots is widening, if anything.

*****

The 1990 conference formally established the Community's Assembly of Representatives, or General Assembly, as the Community's highest authority, 'charged with crystallising the practice of participatory democracy'. It consisted of representatives directly elected by the Community, each representing an average of 200 electors (people over 16). The representatives would be 'incorporated into the communal collectives of each settlement, in order to give a voice to those they represent in decision-making about issues affecting the Community'.
With 5,000 potential voters in the Community, the General Assembly has about 250 members, and is CSM's broadest-based assembly. In principle, General Assemblies are held every three months, although in practice they take place only about half as often. The last one just before our visit was a special assembly to discuss Target 2000. Before each Assembly,

> "there's a process to discuss who will be the delegates and what they are going to propose. Often, before the General Assembly begins, we publish the basic themes that will be discussed at it, so that people can express their opinions."

In between, there are regular and occasional meetings at various levels of leadership.

Two hundred and forty-two delegates attended the July 1991 General Assembly, Juan José tells us. However, his description of the Assembly's current composition looks rather more selective than that envisaged in 1990, based on work areas and social sectors rather than places of residence:

> "all the coordinators, and a delegate for every ten workers, the delegates of the different organised sectors in the Community, such as women, the war-wounded, young people, the elderly, all those who are represented as organised sectors. And the *Junta Directiva*."

In fact, for a community famed for its collectivism, Ciudad Segundo Montes is 'run' by a surprisingly small number of people. Practical policy-making about the big issues affecting the Community rests very largely with the 13-member *Junta Directiva* and with the management of the various *organismos*. Altogether, these total about sixty people.

The *organismos* are the various administrative organisations of the Community. There are ten of them: CODEMO, CODECO, the Bank, Urban Development, Health, Education, Social Communication, External Relations, Communal Services, and Administration (including the San Salvador office). Each *organismo* is headed by a coordinator who works with an executive committee of four or five people. These management teams meet on the first Saturday of each month, 'to coordinate work and look at general comments and suggestions on problems that have occurred'. "Individual *organismos* also hold occasional internal meetings with their workers," says Rosa Elia. "But they happen sporadically, when there's something very important to discuss." The Teachers' Assembly we attended, for example, was part of a special consultation process for Target 2000; all the *organismos* are to hold similar meetings, discussing the same questions.

Juan José insists that the *Junta Directiva* is not the same thing as the group of coordinators managing the various administrative organisations. The latter are appointed, whereas the *Junta Directiva* is a larger body, elected for three years (and including Juan José himself as General Coordinator). However, from what we have seen, there is a big overlap – so big, in fact, that even leaders themselves are not always clear about the distinction.

There is also another, parallel, structure – *Comunal* (Communal Services) – the equivalent of a municipal government. *Comunal* provides services such as public security, environmental protection, sanitation, nurseries, barbers, and social welfare. This last service provides assistance to the 'vulnerable sectors' (lone mothers, the elderly) and offers small loans or grants to help the neediest individuals to start up income-generating projects.

Comunal grew out of the camp committees, the basic form of social organisation at Colomoncagua. Perhaps because of this history, it is now the only structure in CSM to combine service-provision with a geographically-based form of representation involving assemblies and committees at a settlement, or neighbourhood level. In each of the five settlements there is a coordinator, known simply as *el Comunal*, who is a kind of mayor; then there is a general coordinator of *Comunal* who is

Discussion group 11 at the Community's
international conference in 1990.

ESCHR

a member of the Community's *Junta Directiva*. Unlike the other
organisations, which represent only paid employees of the Community,
Comunal has the capacity to represent the whole Community, including
those who are not employed in any Community organisation.

*****

"So we do have a kind of self-government," says Juan José, "but it's still
a real muddle. We need to find ways of regulating participatory
democracy."

Our long afternoon meeting has drifted into informality and welcome
cold beers at the Guacamaya Subversiva cafeteria as the evening sky
deepens and the sultry air cools and softens. We have been joined by Darío
from CODEMO, Dieter, a German volunteer, and Patrick, a Canadian
visitor.

We ask what participatory democracy means at Ciudad Segundo
Montes. How is the leadership going about encouraging people to think
and act for themselves, we ask, given the legacy of dependency?

"That's what decentralisation is all about," says Juan José, "giving the workers more control of production, encouraging individuals to start up their own initiatives..." "But that's economic independence," Dieter breaks in; "and you know, a lot of people think it just means they're being abandoned without any consultation. What people need is the political space to disagree with those policies. I'm not saying the policies are wrong; I'm just saying that freedom to take decisions about your own livelihood – even with financial help – isn't the same thing as access to decision-making about important issues for the Community as a whole. And that's what people want. Many people are really against economic decentralisation; but they see it going ahead anyway, so they feel no one will listen to them if they complain."

If that's true, how does it square with the principle of participatory democracy?

"Well, we have quite a straightforward view on that," Juan José replies. "It should enable people to participate not only in decision-making but also in drawing up proposals. The Teachers' Assembly's a good example: there you had all the teachers discussing the most important issues affecting the Community today – issues where we need to know what people think before we can go forward. And it's all on the record, so we can't ignore it." "That's true," says Dieter; "but the teachers didn't have any say in setting the agenda: they were given a list of questions to consider, and there was no space to raise their own questions."

We remark that nearly all the groups at the Teachers' Assembly thought people were poorly informed by the leadership and wanted more accountability from leaders and more say in how money was being used. One group had even said they couldn't really comment on the quality of the leadership or administration because they had never been told how those structures worked.

"Besides," Dieter adds, "even if all the work areas are consulted in this way, one by one – however good the consultation is – these assemblies still don't reach the people who haven't got community jobs, the so-called *no-estructurados* (unstructured). It's a good word for them, 'unstructured': there's no structure for them, no channel for them to express their views to the leadership. How can they make their voices heard?"

"Well, there's *Comunal*,' says Rosa Elia. "Regarding Target 2000, Communal Services has consulted both Community employees and those who don't work. The five coordinators of Communal Services have been holding their own general assemblies to discuss this with the people in each settlement."

A woman and two elderly men sitting at the next table have been listening with interest. Now Juan José calls over to one of them: "Don Román, weren't you discussing this in the pastoral committee last week?"

"Yes, but we had some doubts. There's a lot that doesn't make sense to us. Some people were asking where all the international aid money goes. No one ever tells us; we just see all these big buildings going up. And meanwhile people in the Community are really poor. But no one ever explains to us why some of the elderly people are given food and some aren't. Is there a list? And then, if you grow a little maize, a few beans, you get cut off the list, as if you were rich. But the *Junta Directiva* never meets with us to explain policies like this, so we can't tell them that even if we grow enough maize to sell a bit, that doesn't mean we've got a glut. We need the money for sugar, coffee, a hat or shoes when the old ones wear out."

Darío ponders this. "Participatory democracy is really pretty new to us," he says finally, "but I think the problem isn't talking about it, it's doing it, it's the practice and experience, and that includes knowledge of what democracy means."

"Then you need political education," says Patrick. "People need to know how their society is run if they're going to participate in it. The education system needs to nurture critical faculties in people but, from what I've seen in the classrooms so far, it's more a matter of rote learning than critical debate."

At the other table Vicenta gives a smile with a lot of weariness in it. "You know, the biggest problem can be just finding the time. I'm on the El Barrial collective of the Christian Mothers' Committee, and we call fortnightly meetings of all the ladies. We go round all the houses reminding them but often only 25 or so will turn up. Everyone's just too busy now."

Román agrees: "People are getting more reluctant to commit themselves to political work. It's the same with pastoral work. People don't want to leave their *milpa*, they don't want to go to lots of meetings anymore. And the whole Community is so much bigger, so much more scattered – it takes longer to get to and from meetings. People haven't got the energy for it."

"So if a problem arises, there's a tendency to think that the way to solve it is just to create a structure to deal with it," says Dieter; "to elect a committee and leave it at that. And that means people never learn leadership skills or confidence; and so the same few leaders will keep getting elected, because they're the ones with the knowledge and the experience – it's a vicious circle!"

*****

This certainly seems true of the current leadership, we reflect, as we trek up to Quebrachos by torchlight, long after the last vehicle has gone. Several of them have been leading the Community since before the repatriation and were simply re-elected at the 1991 Assembly. But how many people in the Community actually want to be running the show? Not everyone is a natural leader, and even at the leadership level few people have the political vision and sophistication of Juan José or Darío. For all the ease with which they manage political vocabulary, most people in the Community are probably content to be led, as long as they can feel sure they will be listened to if they have something to say. The important thing is that the structures or mechanisms allowing their voices to be heard must be guaranteed.

In fact there are really three separate representational mappings of the Community. The first and oldest is that of *Comunal* and reproduces the geographical divisions into sub-camp and colony of the refugee camp. Changes since the repatriation, the different geography, and the imperative of work on subsistence crops in the *milpa* have weakened this structure so that it is no longer the main channel for political participation. The second is organisation by sector – women, young people, the elderly and pastoral; the structures are alive and well, though geographically fragmented, but those active in them feel that they have little say in decision-making, and none at all over expenditure. Finally there is organisation by sector, by employment, which seems increasingly to be the one that counts, although it represents only those with Community jobs. Its power derives from its command of aid money and the fact that its members come together on a daily basis.

The General Assembly in its current form has some serious limitations. There are no mechanisms in place to ensure that its recommendations are carried out by the *Junta Directiva*; on the contrary, the *Junta's* practical and personal power means that it can manipulate the Assembly vote. Also, while in theory it gives all Community members representation, in practice the Assembly is now largely reduced to an assembly of Community employees. The growing gap between those with Community jobs and those without is not only one of wealth but of political power.

There is also the question of the political pluralism in the Community. The current leaders of CSM – and many of its citizens – are people who were doing political work for the FMLN during the war, and several of them clearly regard CSM's incorporation into the municipality of Meanguera as a way of increasing the political strength of the FMLN in the area. Northern Morazán is largely supportive of the FMLN but not unanimously so, and as people move in and out of the zone, it will inevitably become more heterogeneous politically as well as economically. If Juan José's concept of participatory democracy is to become a reality, the Assembly needs to ensure that it represents all people in the Community, eventually also allowing space for the development of political pluralism.

14
Families

"Fifty-four years," says Isidora, deftly sculpting and flattening a maize tortilla as she rotates it between her hands. "Fifty-four years I've been patting out tortillas." She speaks with pride rather than resentment or wearinesss: she is sixty-six years old and has had fourteen children. Eight survive: three joined the FMLN and died in battle, three others died 'natural deaths'. Despite the size of her family, Isidora's household at Quebrachos is now relatively small: besides Isidora herself, there are her husband, her daughter Maribel, who works in the dental surgery, Maribel's husband and their two daughters. Maribel's now-disabled brother, Francisco, who was severely wounded in 1991, lives nearby.

Families are big in rural El Salvador and CSM is no exception. But the Community is also a microcosm of the way the war tore families apart and shattered normal or traditional family patterns. Severe demographic distortion is clear even from a superficial glance at CSM's population structure: of a total population of 7,900, over half (4,223) are children under fourteen, while in the 15-44 age band there are over twice as many women as men. There are just 434 men in the Community aged between 15 and 44 – the age range of those who fought in the war. In effect, a whole generation of men – and some women – has vanished.

The war has resulted in all sorts of atypical family situations: skipped generations, with grandparents bringing up grandchildren; families bringing up war orphans who may or may not be related to them by blood; and most notably households headed by a widow or other single woman, which now account for well over half the total number of households.

This trend is observable anywhere in the country but in the bitterly fought-over FMLN strongholds like Morazán it is acute. The FMLN is estimated to have suffered 15,000 – 20,000 casualties in the course of the war, replacing its entire membership at least twice. "Oh yes," says Isidora, "there's not a family here that hasn't lost at least one person to the war and the repression."

Two of Isidora's own sons were killed in 1980, during the army's first attack on El Mozote. Like many other older couples in the Community, she and her husband both survived and are still together – although the repression and massacres also made many widows among the older generation. Luisa, who works in the External Relations office, tells how soldiers arrived at her mother's house early one morning and killed her father while he sat stripping the sisal from maguey leaves. Over 300 women in CSM are widows – at least one says she has been widowed twice – but hundreds more have simply been parted from husbands or partners by the circumstances of war. Women who went to Colomoncagua spent years apart from combatant partners and not all relationships survived the separation. Other families were divided politically by the conflict, often those who had been well-off before the war. Cipriano Sánchez tells how his landlord's sons joined the FMLN although their father had no sympathy with it; another lad from a rich local family told his parents he was moving to San Salvador to be safe but joined the guerrilla fighters in the mountains instead. Now these families are reuniting, as are parents who fled Morazán with small children, leaving behind teenage sons and daughters who had joined the FMLN ranks.

Despite these violent disruptions, the nuclear family is apparently reasserting itself in CSM. According to the IDEA survey, at the end of 1991 there were 1,121 nuclear families (probably including those headed by a lone mother, although IDEA does not make this clear) and 648 extended families. Only 58 people in the whole Community live alone; there are few childless households. Many families adopted children orphaned in the war or in massacres: Helena at the Quebrachos cafeteria, for instance, has an adopted child as well as her own four and the one she is expecting. Helena's household, in fact, spans four generations, for both her mother and her grandmother (aged 101 and still a practising midwife) live with her. Many second marriages (or consensual unions, which are far more common) were made in Colomoncagua, too.

*****

The IDEA survey records 1,198 mothers and only 417 fathers in the Community, making nearly three mothers to every father. There are 814 women-headed households. A number of women have had children by three or four different fathers, none of them any longer on the scene. Many of the single mothers are widowed (273 according to IDEA); some have husbands or partners awaiting demobilisation or overseas receiving treatment for war injuries. The fortunes of war, however, can't entirely explain why CSM has so many single mothers. Many women told IDEA that they had simply been abandoned 'for one reason or another'.

Young girl washing her baby brother   Jenny Matthews

At lunch in the Cultural Centre we raise these questions with the people at our table: Rosa Elia, who is also the *Junta Directiva* member responsible for women, Luisa, Father Rogelio, and Anna, a foreign worker. Why so many single mothers and 'floating' fathers?

"It's certainly not just a product of the war," Rogelio says. "It's always been this way. But it's clear that the war has distorted men. They've become arrogant and macho. I've had several discussions with ex-combatants about the way they treat women. They talk about emancipation, women's development, but it's just talk. In practice, they don't take women seriously at all."

Anna adds: "And the total dependence on aid in Colomoncagua actually made it easier for men to be irresponsible, too. They didn't have to provide for their families – they couldn't! So they could just flit from woman to woman and not worry about who was going to feed all the babies; and they're still doing it."

Overcrowding also plays a part, Luisa remarks. "Many families are still sharing houses; in some houses there are twelve people living all together, two families to a house."

We ask about the Community's attitude towards single mothers. Are they regarded as a disadvantaged or vulnerable sector?

"I think the Community wants to discourage single motherhood," says Anna. "Take the debate in April about whether the first permanent houses should go to single mothers or not. I think the vote went against the single mothers because the leadership didn't want to give the idea that single mothers were a privileged sector."

But isn't this a case of blaming the victim, of punishing women for having children as though they alone were responsible for conception?

Rosa Elia disagrees. For her, the solution is to promote income-generating projects for single mothers rather than taking a welfare approach, such as preferential access to new houses. But family planning is also very important. "I have two children; the father of my elder son is dead, he died here in 1984; and then in the refuge, I got pregnant with another child, but I stopped there. Since the father didn't want to take any responsibility, we separated. So I work for my children, I give them advice, I bring them up. One is in third grade, he's ten years old, and the other is five. I think life's quite complicated enough with two!"

"But women like you, with education and a good position in the Community, are more able to take your own decisions," Anna objects. "For most young women it's a real double bind. On the one hand, the Community is saying the birthrate has to be brought down, there are too many babies; but on the other hand, you don't become a real woman in this society until you've had a child. Most girls are really keen to have their first baby, and they usually have them by the age of 15 or 16, sometimes even a couple of years younger."

How easy is it to get contraception? "Pretty easy" Anna tells us, "and it's quite widely used. There are condoms and oral contraceptives in all the clinics. A lot of the older women use IUDs, but this is usually when they want to stop childbearing. Women don't use contraception to delay the start of childbearing."

"But we have to reduce the number of children. All through the war, here and in the refuge, we've had a birthrate of around 28 babies a month – nearly one a day – and statistical experts tell us that at this rate we'll have trebled the population in 17 years. We can't allow that to happen.

"I think the church should change its position if it wants more credibility with the population. It ought to say that raising the children is the responsibility of the family, both the man and the woman, a shared responsibility. You can't abandon children; that really is a sin. I reckon the church has a really important educational role in this respect. It's something I've been proposing to the priests and to the Pastoral committees."

It's clear that the Community leadership is concerned about single motherhood; but what is missing from the discussion is any suggestion that irresponsible fathers might be disapproved of or penalised in any way. Rogelio thinks things will have to change, particularly among the demobilised combatants: "In the Frente [FMLN] they learned to take advantage of women combatants. They'd be with one woman one day, another the next. Of course this is nothing new in civilian life; but in the FMLN it was treated as if it were an achievement, a new concept of sexual relations. They tried to justify the idea that sexual relations had nothing to do with emotions or feelings, you had to rationalise them. Now they're going to have to relearn how to live with women and children."

Infidelity isn't the only problem in the family. There's also been an increase in domestic violence, and most people put this down to the return of hard liquor to the Community. Alcohol was strictly forbidden in the closed context of the refugee camp, but here in Morazán it has been impossible to keep it out of the Community. Luisa says: "We only started to allow the sale of beer in the Community last year. But it's not beer that causes the problems; it's the *guaro* (strong cane spirit) people drink down by the river. It comes from the other side of the river, they bring it up here, sometimes they mix it with beer, and that's what gets men drunk."

*****

Twelve years of war have taken not just a physical but a psychological toll of everyone in CSM. Families have been violently torn apart and just as abruptly thrown back together again. The IDEA survey concluded that the experiences they had been through had harmed people's ability to relate to each other:

> "... the possibility of respect, openness to others, and love were frequently blocked by the need to lie at both the personal and the social levels as a mechanism for survival in wartime ...
>
> Within the family, few demonstrations of affection were observed, particularly in the case of couples; this could be explained as a difficulty resulting from the harshness of the ambience of war and repression. Apparently there is little communication within the family: sometimes women said they did not know much about the activities of their partners or their adult sons and daughters."

This seems a rather pessimistic assessment and it is possible that IDEA's researchers did not take full account of people's natural reserve in the presence of strangers, especially in a population such as this which has significant indigenous elements. But it is also true that people's lives here are full of ghosts and there has been little public recognition or commemoration of the bereavement every person in CSM over the age of 12 or 13 has suffered. Anna tells us the story of a woman she knows who lost her husband early in the war and married again in Colomoncagua. Shortly after the repatriation her first husband began to appear in her dreams, reproaching her for remarrying and saying he had waited for her in El Salvador. "It's like what people found here when they returned," Anna says. "Everyone's former lives have got all over-grown, and when you start clearing away the tangle, you find the unburied dead."

15
Schools

"Good morning, young friends, this is Radio Segundo Montes. We're here once again to bring you the programme Children's World, hoping that you will enjoy our broadcast." There follow half a dozen records of twee but jolly children's songs: 'Two Little Chinamen'; 'I sailed to the Island'; etc... Fade-out to a Spanish version of the BeeGees' 'Staying Alive'... "It's 10.26 and we send special greetings to all the children listening to our programme... Now we have for you the story of White Flower: 'Once upon a time there was a very rich queen. She had many castles and much land; and all the jewellery and dresses she wanted. But she had no child...'" The story is a commercial recording read by professional actors.

Children's World is broadcast daily, and sometimes includes the children's own requests, both for music and stories. The announcers are themselves young people, one of them only 13 years old. The radio station has been on the air for two years, and for the last twelve months has been broadcasting on FM, eight hours a day, from 8.00 - 11.30am and 4.00 - 8.00pm. The aim is to reach the whole of northern Morazán, but at present the transmitter is not sufficiently powerful. Programmes include news, cultural material, details of Community projects and Children's World.

Today, Radio Segundo Montes is also broadcasting a programme made by the Community's teachers and addressed to parents. It describes a new initiative to form parents' committees in each settlement, 'to improve the participation of parents in the education of their children.' The Radio has been out to talk to parents and responses are favourable. The programme concludes with a long and detailed debate about the problem of absenteeism.

*****

The Education Offices are housed in a wooden, corrugated-iron roofed hut down the hill from the Cultural Centre. Margarita, an administrator, describes how education is organised. Ciudad Segundo Montes provides kindergarten and primary education to 3,590 children, with schools functioning in each of the five settlements. Children start school at four, spend two years in kindergarten and then go on to primary first grade.

There is no secondary school but there are now seventh grade classes (effectively first year secondary) in each of the settlements, and plans to open eighth and ninth grade in the future.

Nearby, a group of seven to eight year olds sit in the shade on tree roots or stones, chattering noisily and paying little attention to the teacher, a youth of perhaps 17, who is writing on a blackboard leaning against a tree. Several of the children are running around, while another is perched in the fork of a tree, too far away to see or hear properly. Margarita says discipline is quite a problem, as well as absenteeism, which is on the increase. This is the first year when almost every family has begun in earnest to sow maize and beans in their *milpa* plot, and some keep their children off school to work on the land, or to look after younger siblings or animals while the parents go to the *milpa*. The teachers visit families whose children are absent and try to remonstrate with them. 'Education never put food on the table,' say a number of the mothers. Yet, even within the Community, the teachers argue, education is the passport to jobs.

The San Luis school consists of two long wooden huts, each divided into two classrooms. They were only built earlier this year: before that all the classes were in the open air. Even now there are not enough classrooms for all the children in San Luis.

"They don't really provide an ideal environment for the children," says Medardo, one of the teachers. "When it rains, because the roof-overhang is too shallow, the rain comes straight into the classrooms, and we can't teach properly because of the noise of the rain on the corrugated iron. Maybe in the future we will build better ones." A few posters are pinned on the wood-plank walls, and there is a blackboard. Children are squeezed three or four to a tiny bench surely designed for two, drawn up to narrow tables barely 18 inches wide, with a shelf underneath. There are very few books, and scarcely any writing materials. The only light comes from the gap between the walls and roof, which is protected by wire mesh.

*****

The Community employs and pays *educadores populares*, 'popular' or community teachers – as opposed to what they consistently term the 'traditional' teachers in the government schools. Many of them are as young as 15 or 16 and none has completed secondary school. Most teach either a morning or an afternoon shift and come to the Teachers' Centre in the afternoon for teacher training and collective lesson preparation. In the evenings some teach adult classes, while others return to San Luis as

One of the 3,590 children now educated
in Community schools

Jenny Matthews

pupils in seventh grade. On Wednesdays there are training sessions for the teachers in subjects like dance, sport and speech.

Teaching is based on methods developed in the refugee camp in Colomoncagua and inspired by the work of the Brazilian educationalist Paolo Freire. In nine years of exile, and with minimal resources, the level of illiteracy among the refugees was reduced from over 50% to about 17%. At the same time, a large proportion of the best young pupils worked for some time as educators, receiving additional education and training, and the experience of teaching not only other children, but adults of their parents' and grandparents' generations. While some remain teachers after the repatriation, many have gone on to take up other responsibilities within the Community. It is a long-standing complaint of the education organisers that their best teachers are continually poached for jobs in other structures of the Community.

At the Teachers' Centre, we sit down to chat with some of these young teachers: Clarisa, Reina, Medardo and Santos. Three of them are in their early twenties while Reina is a little older, perhaps thirty. She went to school for four years in Torola before the war.

"It was very different there. I think the popular education we give here is much better. We offer more guidance and the children learn more. Some of the teachers in the government schools teach like us, but most don't.

In the government education system they believe that education is for the few, so that families with a bit more money can 'buy the grade' for their children. If you can't pay for the grade, you have to repeat the year. So children from families with money get on while those from poor families get left behind. Sometimes children in third grade whose parents can pay will be put straight up to sixth grade even if they haven't a clue."

We ask about the average grade children in the Community will attain. "Sixth grade," says Santos. The others all agree. "That's much higher than the average in the countryside in El Salvador, which is third or even second grade."

"There's a good chance," says Clarisa, "that the children will go on to seventh or eighth grade, as we improve the programme. If the government would recognise our education system, then children who get to seventh grade here could go elsewhere to continue studying."

"Where?" we ask.

"Well," says Medardo, "they've got up to ninth grade at the government school in Perquín. Otherwise, there's Osicala or San Francisco Gotera. I'm studying seventh grade myself here. If I get a chance, I would like to go on. I think all of us would. The international advisers could provide secondary classes for us. There are enough children here for a complete secondary school."

*****

Legal recognition by the government is a key problem for the Community, affecting all its services, but especially health and education. With education there is a double problem: recognition and accreditation of the popular teachers; and validation of the grades awarded since repatriation in the Community's schools, and before that in the refugee schools at Colomoncagua. As Mercedes, who is responsible for education on the *Junta Directiva*, tells us:

"Under the Peace Accords, the state is obliged to take over responsibility for some of the services in the Community. So we've made some proposals. If they are not agreed, we won't let the State interfere in our services. We had a meeting with the Minister of Education and then she came and visited our schools. We told her we wanted our popular teachers and our pupils' education recognised. After all the illiteracy our teachers have helped to eradicate, it's not fair that we should have to say to them, 'thanks very much, now you can go home. You're going to be replaced by qualified teachers.' They've got a right to be recognised.

The Minister said 'No: I have 2,000 fully qualified teachers who are unemployed. It would create a political problem for us.' When she went back to the capital, she gave a press conference, and in the newspapers the next day there was a photo of her with me and a group of children under the trees, under a headline '167 schools to be opened in Morazán'. The name Ciudad Segundo Montes wasn't even mentioned. As far as they are concerned, we don't exist. Anyway, it's a lie. They haven't offered a single thing. All they're offering are 35 qualified teachers. Can you imagine! We have 140 teachers in Ciudad Segundo Montes alone! It's just crumbs they're offering! A commission from the San Miguel regional office of the Ministry of Education came here a couple of weeks ago, and told us they'd come to accredit the children in grades one to three. They were armed with tests for the children to do. We asked them how they could bring

ready-made tests to evaluate the children without knowing what
we've been doing.' In the end we refused to let them carry out the
tests. We told them it wouldn't resolve our problems at all, it was just
going to set us back.

We've tried to bring our own curriculum programmes into line
with the Ministry's materials. But we want flexibility for our schools,
not a fixed programme, so that each time there are changes in the
Community, we can change the education a bit to match. We base our
teaching on the Community projects. In maths, for example, we refer
to the cattle project: if the cows produce so many litres of milk and
we sell it at so much a litre to the Community nurseries, etc. We
always relate the teaching to our immediate reality."

*****

Meanguera is clearly visible from the Cultural Centre at San Luis, down
below in the valley. You get to it by taking the turning off the tarmac road
and walking through the Hatos II settlement. It must have been rather an
elegant village, though much of it was abandoned or destroyed during the
war. The church, whitewashed and squat, has a design of blue flowers
painted on its door. Opposite, a woman is living and running a shop in
the old community hall, a fine building with a high ceiling and glossy red-
and-green-tiled floor. The old town hall is a roofless building on the little
high street, sharing premises with the post office, whose sign still swings
idly from a ruined doorway. This was the administrative centre of the
municipality in which Ciudad Segundo Montes stands today.

Meanguera is where the new community intersects with the old
political and administrative structures of the country. There has been talk
of CSM trying to get recognition as a new municipality, but that would
probably be harder than accepting the status quo and attempting to control
it. There is a serious dilemma, however: in return for integration into the
municipality and government recognition, services and funding, the
Community would almost certainly have to relinquish some of its
autonomy. Meanwhile CSM is hedging its bets, cultivating good relations
with the mayor, gradually repopulating the old town and sharing some
of its services with the people there.

The point is neatly illustrated by the education system at Meanguera.
There are two schools. One is an official government primary school. It
has two qualified teachers, but only a handful of pupils. The other school

is run by CSM, and staffed by popular teachers from the Community, and has 29 pupils. CSM, however, provides the food for school dinners for both schools. According to Rosa, one of the CSM teachers in Hatos:

"The traditional [= government] teachers arrived and set up a parent-teacher committee with some of the people who support them. They are very negative towards the Segundo Montes style of education.We said it would be good if we could come to an agreement and work in coordination, and that we had no wish to make problems for them... When enrolment day came nearly all the families enrolled their children with us."

Neftalí teaches in the CSM school at Meanguera:

"People in Meanguera are quite divided along religious lines. The families that send their children to the government school go to the meetings of the parent-teacher committee. You can pick them out because the women wear the head-scarves that the Protestants use. When they have their meetings, it's just those people. The Catholics are with the CSM school. The division is really clear, but it's not right."

Concha, who works in the CSM office in San Salvador, but whose family lives in Meanguera, puts it differently:

"The difference between the two schools is more political than religious. The government teachers accuse Ciudad Segundo Montes of giving 'guerrilla classes'. But the religious divide is rather by family; most of those who stayed in the town during the war were evangelicals who supported the armed forces. They're the ones who tend to send their children to the ministry schools.

But as more and more families from CSM have come back to Meanguera village, there's been less argument... They've seen some of the positive results of the Community. For instance our clinic is the only health service around."

Returning to San Luis, we make our way down the dusty road from the Cultural Centre. On the veranda of the Teachers' Centre, trainee teachers, in their uniforms, are dancing sedately to traditional marimba music on the veranda. This is a dance workshop. Below the San Luis school we see a large crowd of children intensely gazing up at a screen propped up in the open air. They are watching *Tortugas Ninja* – Teenage Mutant Hero Turtles – on the Community's only television set.

16
Colomoncagua Revisited

The border between northern Morazán and the Honduran department of Intibucá is formed by a small river, the Río Negro. Travelling from Segundo Montes to the village of Colomoncagua, you come upon the cool, quiet little gully quite suddenly, not far beyond the Torola turnoff, and ford the river (with more or less difficulty, depending on whether the season is wet or dry) on a dreadful road that is all rocks where it is not mud.

Borders are often a sort of cultural no-man's-land belonging to both the nations they separate and to neither. This one is politically blurry too. An area containing Colomoncagua and a large tract of northern Morazán is one of several pockets of territory disputed by El Salvador and Honduras since the four-day-long 'Football War' of 1969. This war was not really about football at all but about land hunger in both countries. Here there is no border post, yet you soon know you're in another country: where on the Salvadorean side the road winds through all-but-deserted hills punctuated by a few ruins, once safely in Honduras it is lined with small houses and farms, the low, russet-tiled roofs of adobe cottages peeping up above brilliant tangles of orange lantana, narrow paths meandering away to fenced fields and gardens. On this side of the border you see mules with their gable-shaped packs laden with sacks of grain or piles of wood. Cowboy-hatted peasants in fake Lacoste shirts ride horses. Under the protecting mountains it is a villagey landscape, almost picturesque. This is how northern Morazán must have looked for centuries, until the war. When you see this ancient domesticity you realise how much Morazán has lost.

Another country, but the same place. The notorious rivalry between El Salvador and Honduras becomes a good deal less clear-cut when seen up close. Like most borders, this one has always had a floating population for whom artificial political boundaries are rarely an obstacle to local commerce or kinship. By 1969 as many as 300,000 Salvadoreans had settled in Honduras, forming about 20 per cent of Honduras' rural population. Some of them owned Honduran land. Many Salvadoreans who fled into Honduras in the early 1980s knew the old trade routes across the border or had acquaintances or relatives living on the Honduran side.

The village of Colomoncagua marked the beginning of exile for the 8,000 people who populated Colomoncagua refugee camp. A refugee bulletin of the time records the first days in Honduras:

"When we arrived at Colomoncagua we were all hungry, especially the children. Juanita, a woman from the church charity, CARITAS, helped us get some grain so we could make hot cereal for the children. In the church they gave us blankets and we went off to a shelter in a house where only the walls were standing. We covered the top just enough to be able to stay there.

People from the village invited us to their houses and others brought us food for the children. On Sunday they brought us a few pounds of sorghum and corn. Little things, but a gesture of goodwill towards us."

In the 1980s, this had always seemed a sad backwater of a place, its economy and society misshapen by the presence of the army and international organisations. The scruffy little cafés were kept afloat by the custom of the internationals. On market days, foreign visitors would buy the village out of fruit and vegetables to take up to the refugee camp. UNHCR supplies seldom included such treats and the refugees' collective kitchen gardens, however lovingly tended, could not feed one thousand, let alone eight. Servicing the camp provided business for local carpenters and plumbers, contracted to fix up houses in the village where the internationals stayed. On the other hand, the refugee camp was the only place beyond La Esperanza, at least three hours drive back into Honduras, where a vehicle could be repaired, and the refugees' mechanics shop regularly repaired local people's vehicles for a low fee.

Colomoncagua is still a backwater, but less of a garrison town nowadays. It used to have a customs and immigration post, but that closed down with the departure of the Salvadorean refugees, the UNHCR unit, and the many foreign workers who were only there because the refugees were. Nowadays this is not an official entrance to Honduras. The only authority you have to report to is the army: it was always the army that ruled here, anyway. Its post is manned by an officious lieutenant and two listless teenage soldiers, one of whom comes out to ask us our names and business, stirring his lunchtime rice in a saucepan. "What do you want to go up there for?" he says. "There's nothing there any more."

The young soldier is right. The Colomoncagua camps, a mile or two beyond the village, are now utterly deserted, except for a local family's farmlet in a pleasant glade just inside the old entrance. Their house is new and has clearly been built since the camps were dismantled. The access road, completely neglected, is worn down to the rock and almost impossible to drive along. No sign survives of the *tranca*, the checkpoint where the road was physically barred by a tree-trunk pole across it, but the foreign workers remember its location exactly, after the hours spent there arguing with Honduran soldiers before they could get in or out. The chequerboard of tin roofs that sparkled at you in the sun as you came down the hill into the Limón I subcamp is gone. All you can see now of what was once a bustling (if beleaguered) community of eight subcamps covering several hundred acres are a few foundations of buildings, and many of these were reportedly destroyed by the Honduran military after the refugees left, in a belated search for FMLN 'bunkers'.

The only monuments to the Salvadorean refugees' nine years of occupation are three little cemeteries nestling up on hillsides above the road. Each is marked by a large white wooden cross, inscribed *'Refug-iados de Colomoncagua !!viven siempre en nuestro pueblo!!'* ('Refugees of Colomoncagua: you will always be amongst us'). One of the crosses has a bullet hole in it. The graves, set among grass, are marked by small crosses leaning at jaunty angles, painted sky blue or turquoise, the colours of death in this region, with the names pricked out in nail-holes. Some have flowers planted at the foot, and entwined round many crosses are the remains of wreaths of wire and flowers, like little crowns of thorns. These are places of extraordinary tranquillity and spirituality. It is as if each is cradled in a bubble of peaceful solitude quite different from the eery nostalgia of the rest of the site.

*****

What distinguished Colomoncagua from the other Salvadorean refugee camps along the Honduran border was the homogeneity of its population. Whereas refugees in Mesa Grande and San Antonio, the two other large camps, came from several different places in El Salvador, practically everyone who fled to Colomoncagua was from Morazán. People from Morazán fled south as well as north, to other Salvadorean towns like Osicala, which has a significant outer 'suburb' of displaced people's dwellings, or to San Francisco Gotera, where large camps of displaced people grew up on the outskirts of the town, and beyond. While there was no exact correlation between people's political views and the direction of their flight, FMLN sympathisers were more likely to cross into Honduras, where control by the Salvadorean armed forces was less direct.

This tendency increased as the war dragged on, consolidating the political unity of the Honduran camp. The displaced camps at Gotera, by contrast, were riddled with informers and army personnel were constantly in and around the camps and recruiting from them; they were therefore a far more hostile environment for anyone known to favour the FMLN or any anti-government organisation.

Visitors to Colomoncagua were surprised not only by the camp's liveliness and air of purpose but by its sheer size and spread. By the late-1980s there were eight main sub-camps, each governed by a group consisting of leaders of the different work areas (health, education, and so on) and 'sectors' (women, children, elderly people, youth) and coordinators of the *colonias* or neighbourhoods into which the subcamp was itself divided; leaders chosen from these governing groups formed the overall camp leadership.

At first the refugees were housed in tents and various ramshackle structures of timber, sheet metal, and plastic sheeting, but these were gradually replaced with barrack-like timber buildings. Many of these were public or communal buildings: kitchens (one of the refugees' first collective undertakings, later used as 'nutrition centres' where elderly people, pregnant and nursing mothers, and babies received extra food rations), clinics, schools, meeting rooms, workshops. Family dwellings were similar, each *carpa* subdivided to house more than one family. (The refugees continued to call the long wooden cabins *carpas*, which literally means 'tent', long after the actual tents had disappeared.) The international volunteers who worked with the refugees had little houses scattered among the refugees' dwellings, although they also had accommodation below in the village – at tense times the volunteers' presence in the camp was seen (not always correctly) as valuable protection for the refugees against incursions by Honduran soldiers. There were chapels – big, airy spaces roofed but not walled – grain stores, poultry and small livestock enclosures, electric generators. By 1988 power lines were even beginning to be built in some subcamps. Viewed from the checkpoint, which overlooked the entire camp area, this expanse of buildings and pathways among the sparse pine woods gave the impression of a small town – and indeed this was one of the largest concentrations of people in this remote part of Honduras. But the refugees were not permitted to leave their little town and were given no agricultural land to work.

The Colomoncagua refugees' achievements – the strong social organisation, the impressive advances in literacy, the workshops training peasants in a variety of new, non-agricultural skills – became legendary. But what most impressed the refugees' supporters – and infuriated the authorities to the extent that they were once dubbed 'the Khmer Rouge of Central America' – was this formidable organisation and unity. From 1983 onward, they successfully resisted a series of plans either to repatriate them against their will or to relocate them further into Honduras, arguing both that El Salvador continued to be too dangerous to live in and that their departure from Colomoncagua would leave the way clear for the Honduran military to complete a string of bases along the border from which to collaborate with their Salvadorean counterparts against the FMLN. They protested frequently *en masse* against harassment by the Honduran army and regularly denounced cooperation between the Salvadorean and Honduran armed forces near the border. In June 1988, dissatisfied with the steadily deteriorating quality of health care they were receiving from the international organisation, Médecins Sans Frontières (MSF), they mounted a hunger strike and eventually forced MSF out of the camp. And they made excellent international contacts, becoming very sophisticated at dealing with aid agencies, solidarity groups, and human rights organisations.

The Honduran and Salvadorean authorities and the US embassies in both countries insisted throughout the war that the refugee camps in Honduras, and especially Colomoncagua, were rearguard bases or safe havens for the FMLN. For the refugees themselves, it was a question of family relationships and the struggle to keep the family together and protect its more vulnerable members, the women, children, and older people. Most of the refugees had relatives fighting in the FMLN, or supported or identified with organisations, such as the Christian base communities, opposed to the Salvadorean government. That, after all, was the main reason why they had been persecuted. But while there was undoubtedly a good number of highly politicised people in Colomoncagua, there were also many whose political awareness was created in the harsh reality of the camp – the 'prison without walls', as the refugees came to call it.

Women in particular acquired leadership capacities and discovered untapped reserves of strength and confidence in themselves. As one refugee said:

"We never chose to be in the refuge, it was a prison. But we had to learn things we'd never even thought about before, we had to learn how to have meetings and organise other people, and it changed us. We'll never be quite the same again."

*****

The experience of Colomoncagua gave the refugees three things: new skills and knowledge, a sense of unity through collective practical and political work, and the confidence to campaign for what they wanted and persist until they got it. The refugees themselves described the experience as a 'school for the future' and stressed that what they had learned would be of great value not only for themselves but for the whole country when the time came to reconstruct Salvadorean society at the end of the war. They had built a unique model of social relations, community services, and production which they believed could be the basis for a new kind of social and economic development in El Salvador.

But the impossibility of agricultural production in the camp reinforced near-total dependence on aid, while the camp's insecurity and the hostility of the Honduran army meant that the population had to be firmly united behind their leaders and prepared to obey an almost military discipline, simply for safety's sake. For Darío Chicas, CSM's head of Production, these factors led to a potentially dangerous passivity:

> "The refuge was a concentration camp, and it generated all these abnormal situations: for instance, there was no money, and there was so much aid. And that distorted people's attitudes to values like responsibility and independence. And if you add to that the vertical structures of power in the Community, you find that people's creative faculties and initiative dry up. The structures of organisation in Colomoncagua and the way they worked were vertical, people tended to take instructions or orders from people higher up. And so they went into abeyance. They lost those creative aspects of the personality, their initiative, and people fell into a sort of torpor that is still reflected in many aspects of life in CSM."

Much more than the other refugee communities, the Colomoncagua refugees brought home with them not only the transforming experience of the camp (and indeed its physical infrastructure), but also the aid agencies that had supported them for so many years: their ideas, their projects, and even some of their personnel. Several international workers at CSM have been with the community since the mid-1980s or even earlier. This ensured continuity of support from the agencies, but it also made the community slow to adapt to its new circumstances. There was a tendency simply to transpose the 'Colo' model, unmodified, to Morazán.

If it had worked – and attracted funding – in Colo, it would work and attract funding in CSM.

At first, this did work. Indeed, there seemed no alternative but to replicate the Colo model in Morazán, where conditions for successful agriculture were if anything worse than when they had left it. The repatriation to Meanguera was based on the idea of creating an urban community that would mesh with and complement the existing rural communities of Morazán. The aid agencies, who had admired what the refugees were doing in Colo, devoted very large amounts of money to helping them do it all over again. It soon became clear, however, that the experience of Colomoncagua could not be automatically or schematically translated to CSM. For all its danger and hardship, Colomoncagua was a capsule sealed off from ordinary life.

*****

The sun is setting as we repass the abandoned checkpoint. A couple of men leading a cow along the road down to the village give us that 'crazy-foreigners' look. So does the young soldier when we check out at the military post. "See anything?" he asks, adding, without being asked his opinion, "Pack of Communists, they were. We were glad to see the back of them."

Cleotilde remembers their farewell as the first group of refugees filed through Colomoncagua village on their way home on 18 November 1989:

"The army had told the people of Colomoncagua to stay inside and shut their doors. But the people didn't pay any attention ... when they heard that we were coming and that we were going to El Salvador, they came out into the streets to see us and say good-bye, and lots of the women cried ... some people wanted to say something to us but couldn't, they were too full of emotion. Yes, some of the people were really sympathetic to us."

17
Perquín

The further north you go, the higher. Perquín is 1,200 metres above sea level. From Quebrachos you gain 600 metres in height along a sinuous road pitted with bomb craters and subsiding from neglect. The hillside drops steeply away to the left, revealing plane upon plane of a landscape that becomes more majestic with each boneshaking yard.

The bus taking us to Perquín seems even more antiquated than most. It creeps upward towards the pine belt, unsteadily but doggedly, like a drunk determined to get home before dawn. It stalls frequently. Each time it does, people shake their heads sorrowfully and say, 'it won't make it'. But each time it starts off again gamely, grumbling and heaving and rattling. As the road winds upwards, the air becomes cooler and fresher and the first pine trees punctuate the skyline. The hillsides are scarred by rocky outcrops and waterfalls gleam here and there. Just before Perquín we pass La Tejera where you turn off for the Honduran border. There are several small sawmills by the road, with piles of freshly-sawn planks and mounds of pine-scented sawdust.

Along the road, women are spinning sisal, the tough string-like yarn made from the fibrous maguey leaves. The fibres are a beautiful creamy colour, with the silky texture of coarse hair. The spinning process appears (deceptively) to consist of grasping a handful of fibres more or less at random and walking backwards, whereupon, as if by magic, the fibres become incorporated into an ever-lengthening yarn. Two women are working on a double strand which is now about a hundred yards long, stretched out along the roadside and supported at intervals by forked sticks that keep it a couple of feet off the ground. At the other end, a little boy is winding the yarn on a simple wooden spinning wheel.

Before the war, sisal and the things made from it – hammocks, baskets and bags, coffee sacks – were often the only income-generating products for subsistence farmers. As Don Virgilio, one of the older citizens of Ciudad Segundo Montes, likes to recall:

"Nearly everyone had their little plot of land and their crops, especially maguey; you use it to make string, rope, hammocks, baskets, all those things. Morazán was where the most fibre was produced, and we used to supply other provinces. In the coffee season, factories used to buy lots of the fibre and make it into sacks for coffee; it's really strong and durable, just a bit scratchy."

Now some people in CSM are beginning to grow maguey again; but it is a slow-growing perennial plant that takes three years to mature, so maguey planted in 1990, soon after the return, is only just ready to harvest.

*****

Perquín was nothing special before the war. It was not a municipal or district centre. Other villages such as Jocoaitique and Joateca were bigger and more important. Probably its main significance was its position right at the end of the only paved road north. It has a special place in the history of the war, however, for it was the first town of any size taken by the FMLN, in August 1981. Today Perquín is the regional administrative centre for northern Morazán, housing the headquarters of the various community organisations of the zone. The FMLN, in the process of converting itself into a political party in 1992, has an office here. On the edge of the village is one of the assembly camps for FMLN combatants awaiting demobilisation. Here too is the home of Radio Venceremos – although these days the station broadcasts more often from San Salvador than from its historical cradle in Morazán.

The presence of the FMLN camp has made Perquín a revolutionary tourist village, with a captured small tank in pride of place at one side of the square, a small shop where flirtatious young *compas* (former combatants) sell scarves, T-shirts and the latest books on FMLN history, surrounded by red-and-white banners. On one side of the church, a cartoon-style mural commemorating five centuries of Latin American resistance depicts the continent in the talons of a yellow-haired female figure who looks suspiciously like Margaret Thatcher. The end wall bears a fine mural in honour of the assassinated archbishop, Mgr Romero, repainted in 1991 after soldiers whitewashed out the original one night. In a large, new cafeteria run by the Morazán development organisation, PADECOMSM, uniformed and plain-clothed *compas* drink cokes and coffee with earnest volunteers and interview-hunting journalists from Barcelona, Toronto, Oakland or Auckland. Cameras abound. But all this is grafted onto an enduringly traditional rootstock visible in the layout of the village around its square and church, the steep streets cobbled in sharp-edged grey stones, the adobe houses where elderly folk look out warily from the shade of deep porches at the passing parade of the young, the uniformed, and the foreign.

Perquín church mural commemorating the
assassinated archbishop, Mgr Romero.

Mike George

*****

Our first port of call is the office of PADECOMSM, the Association for
the Development of the Communities of Morazán and San Miguel.
PADECOMSM was founded in April 1988 to represent and promote the
interests of the civilian communities of the region. Initially formed by the
local councils of 55 communities, it now covers well over 60 communities
in Morazán and northern San Miguel, and is recognised as the
representative grouping of communities in northern Morazán. Its office
in Perquín is large and cool, with rooms that open onto a cloisterlike
veranda, enclosing a central courtyard planted with flowering shrubs and
rambling bougainvillaea. Two members of the executive council, Santos
and Marcial, greet us in a room where agricultural hand tools and boxes
of medical supplies stacked in corners and on shelves coexist happily with
a computer and piles of documents on the desk. On the wall behind them
is a large map of Morazán detailing even the tiniest hamlets.

Although the origins of PADECOMSM, as Marcial explains, lie in the
community councils created in the mid-1980s, its inspiration is to be
found further back, in the ideas of sharing and community life promoted

by the popular church in the Christian base communities and in the pre-war rural cooperative movement. These values and the ways of organising that went with them began to resurface in northern Morazán as early as mid-1983, when pastoral work was resumed with the aim of reunifying the fragmented civilian population and 'restoring a sense of community', as Father Miguel Ventura put it.

The zone had never been completely depopulated. Between 10,000 and 20,000 civilians stayed behind for much if not all of the 1980s. FMLN control of the land north of the river was by no means total, and while the army could not often get in overland from the south, it regularly attacked from the air. According to a survey carried out by PADECOMSM in 1990, at least 49 communities in the region were destroyed or largely depopulated by the war. Government forces waged a relentless war of attrition on the civilians who refused to flee:

"We were only able to survive by staying a few days here, a few days there... there'd be a few months between operations, [when] the people who'd stayed put, all dispersed, would come out of hiding and work for a bit, grow something to eat. And when the next operation came, the people went back again to where they were a bit safer, where the army wouldn't find them and their families. And each time they'd start again on the scorched earth, and the army would burn it all again. They kept on burning the houses and the crops over and over again... That's why you see hardly any houses round here; where there were houses, now there's just scrub."

But by the mid-1980s, as the main war fronts moved back towards the towns, the civilians in northern Morazán gained a breathing space and community councils, women's groups, and Christian base communities began to appear. Among the earliest groups to spring up again were the women's groups. The women of Nuhuaterique, for instance, made an important gesture of collective defiance in 1983, when they refused army orders to wash FMLN slogans off the walls of their village.

Over the following years the communities slowly began to produce food again, to provide some health care and basic education, to make contact with humanitarian agencies and to campaign with increasing openness and confidence for recognition as a legitimate non-combatant population, insisting on their autonomy from the FMLN. The formation of PADECOMSM as a federation was largely a formalisation and public declaration of something that had already been happening for some years. But the federation's potential for coordination and joint action immediately boosted the communities' assertiveness. "If the army touches one member of our communities, now they'll have 25,000 of us to answer to, not just one person or one family," said a woman leader from one of the communities at the inauguration ceremony in San Salvador.

Between 1988 and 1991 PADECOMSM started literacy teaching in many communities and reactivated dozens of schools that had been closed for years. By the end of 1990 42 schools had reopened and PADECOMSM could boast 72 popular educators working in its communities. It opened or reopened health posts. It brought large tracts of abandoned land back into cultivation through a programme of supplying peasant farmers with fertilisers. It set up a reafforestation programme in 1988 to heal some of the ecological damage inflicted by two years of drought on top of eight years of war. It runs an Agricultural Training School at San Fernando.

PADECOMSM works closely with the Women's Communal Movement of Morazán (MCM), with which it shares some projects. However, MCM is an independent women's organisation with its own committees in Perquín and in fifteen rural communities. It is very clear about the need to run its own projects with women, such as community shops, soya growing and the blackberry jam project. Blackberries grow wild in the highest, coolest parts of these mountains, up by the Honduran border and it is women who harvest them. Their jam, sold through MCM, is delicious, but expensive in relation to local incomes so it is mostly bought by foreign visitors.

During the 1980s, here as in the refugee camps, widows and spouses of combatants found themselves thrust into new roles and responsibilities. Many women began to work the land for the first time. The new community structures gave more opportunities for women to play a management role and to participate more actively in community affairs. However, MCM leaders feel there is a long way to go before women are fully incorporated into the decision-making and planning of PADECOMSM projects, and are concerned that the return of peace, and the return of men to ordinary life, will block that process.

Thanks to PADECOMSM, civilians in the zone were able to stay alive during the war, to subsist, and even to begin to enjoy themselves. In August 1988, Perquín celebrated its patron saint's day. The two days of celebrations consisted of a football tournament with six teams from local communities, a Celebration of the Word (liturgy of the popular Catholic Church) led by the Perquín pastoral team, a traditional religious procession involving several hundred people, and a dance to the music of three local bands. A bulletin reporting the event notes laconically that the army's presence 'limited' the evening events somewhat since it prevented the arrival of fourteen other bands who were to take part in a musical competition. Only a month before, the communities around Torola held similar events to mark its saint's day. Miguel Ventura celebrated Mass, and the dance lasted till two in the morning.

*****

Morazán has a short tradition of left-wing sympathy and popular mobilisation. Until the late seventies, its isolation was extreme and its people passive and uncomplaining. In large measure, it was the repression itself that caused people to take a political stance. However, there is no doubt that this degree of organisation by the civilian population could not have been possible – at least in its early stages – without the protection and support of the ERP, the branch of the FMLN operating in Morazán.

In the early stages of the war the ERP, with its heavy emphasis on the military side of the liberation struggle, did tend to see the civilian population only in terms of its potential as combatant material or logistical support. As time went on the ERP increasingly acknowledged the civilian population's need – and right – to exist and operate autonomously. In fact, this became inevitable as the air war from the mid-1980s made it impossible for the guerrillas to defend large expanses of territory and protect a settled civilian population. Meanwhile, young people in Morazán continued to join the guerrilla forces voluntarily throughout the war, despite high casualties, as soon as they were old enough to do so – often at 13 or 14. According to Marisol Galindo, an FMLN leader who was active in political work in Morazán for much of the war, joining the FMLN was an aspiration for young people in Morazán, so that when the offensive of 1989 was announced, many teenagers immediately joined the ranks. A high percentage of ex-combatants are under 21.

However, as the community organisations gained more autonomy and as more people returned to the zone in the later 1980s, it became possible for opponents of the FMLN and even government informers to enter the communities. One of the evangelical Protestant sects, which were widely regarded as pro-government during the war, has a large church in Perquín itself, and the re-opened school is said to be strongly influenced by the right-wing government party, ARENA.

*****

Ciudad Segundo Montes is not a member of PADECOMSM but the two organisations have always collaborated closely. PADECOMSM played a crucial role in the repatriation process, inspecting the site proposed for the new Community and joining in the negotiations over it, bringing lorries to the border on the Salvadorean side to meet the returning refugees, and planting extra maize for the returnees. The returnees paid for this help by pooling the US$50 resettlement grants given to each person by UNHCR. "We organised the production of staple foods for the refugees when they came back from Colomoncagua", Santos explains,

> "since they couldn't begin doing agricultural work as soon as they came back, and in any case they wouldn't have had a crop for several months. Also, there were many people in CSM who had no experience of agricultural work, either because they were too young to have worked before leaving El Salvador in 1980-81, or because they were elderly women who had never worked in the *milpa*."

Perhaps most important of all, PADECOMSM joined the returnees in the negotiations with both the army and the FMLN over access to the zone and the agreement on rebuilding the Torola bridge. Throughout 1990 and 1991 all the zone's community organisations protested as one against the roadblocks and against human rights violations by the armed forces in the zone.

For its part, CSM has put some of the skill and experience gained in Colomoncagua at the disposal of northern Morazán. Soon after repatriation popular educators from among the returnees went into several neighbouring communities linked to PADECOMSM to teach literacy; CSM services such as the clinics, shops, and vehicle repair shop were opened up to the zone as they became established, and CSM runs a 'SuperMontes' general store in Perquín. PADECOMSM and CSM have a joint reafforestation project and cooperate on attempts to control further environmental damage in the region.

Overall, the return of the refugees has clearly been of benefit to the whole zone. The presence of 8,000 extra people with highly-developed skills and an impressive record of getting their own way with authorities has strengthened the zone a great deal and helped give the PADECOMSM communities greater confidence. Nonetheless, the relationship between PADECOMSM and CSM is not always easy. Fr Rogelio remarks that the return of the refugees threw open a door to international aid and attention. But, for a while, Ciudad Segundo Montes eclipsed the rest of the zone:

"Every organisation tends to hoard things a bit. It's always a bit harder to share when you have to start looking beyond your own patch to the development of the rest of the zone ... There's been some jealousy because CSM has received so much aid. Even when aid came for pastoral work – prayerbooks, exercise books, pens and pencils, that sort of thing – it came for CSM. You couldn't help thinking, is this the only community round here? What about the others? How come this community has managed to get its hands on so much of the solidarity?"

Donor agencies are now realising the need to spread their funds more evenly across the zone if balanced economic development and harmony between the communities are to be achieved. But in the end, comfortable coexistence between neighbouring communities in Morazán and CSM may just be a question of time. As more people move out of CSM or commute between one community and another, there is bound to be cross-fertilisation at many levels, blurring the edges between CSM and other communities. Whatever the institutional relationship is like, the informal movement and contact between CSM and other communities may be the true catalyst for integration in the end. Family bonds weave a denser and more durable fabric than any number of organisational links planned in offices and on paper. According to Marisol Galindo, the integration of CSM into PADECOMSM structures "will come about through the communities' day-to-day experience".

18
Workers

On a bluff above the main road at Quebrachos, a small housing estate is taking shape. It is called Copinolar and will contain 30 to 35 small houses of adobe and cement block with tiled roofs. About 120 people are working here, in teams of 10 to 13, erecting the shells of the houses; the roofs, doors and windows will be put in later by the carpenters. The workers are digging deep foundation trenches, filling them with boulders, mixing the cement that will set the boulders into place, pounding down hard earth floors with long-handled wooden mallets. About half of them are women. They are working in broad-brimmed hats and the women are wearing light dresses as well as the ubiquitous blue rubber flipflops, despite the heaviness of the work.

In a corner of the site is a timber shed containing piles of equipment – pickaxes, bags of cement, wheelbarrows – and a table at which two women are working. Ana is a clerk and Marina keeps control of equipment and materials. Clipboards with lists of people and materials hang on the wall behind them.

"Do women do all kinds of jobs in construction?" we ask.

"Yes, pretty much, except for bricklaying. They're not fully trained yet, still learning."

"What about carpentry?"

"No, not yet. But we hope to have some women carpenters in due course."

We ask whether any of the team leaders are women. "No," Ana replies.

"Why not?"

Ana isn't quite sure. "We've sometimes had women team leaders. But the people in charge here are supposed to have a bit more experience. They have to know how to mix cement, lay bricks, and measure up, and the women don't know much about these things."

Both women are aware that building is not a woman's job outside CSM. "In factories where they make tiles and bricks and that," says Marina, "I've seen a couple of women, but that's all. In the electronics factories they're all women – women are cleverer with their hands and more patient. It's been great for capitalism because women always get paid less money for more work."

"But here in CSM, do they pay everyone the same?"

"Oh yes," they both assure us.

"And do the men have trouble accepting that?

This provokes a chuckle. "At first there were a few grumbles but not any more."

Is it difficult being in responsible positions over men and telling them what to do? "Not really," says Ana; "they know the score." But Marina isn't so sure: "Men are sometimes more willing to take orders from another man than from a woman."

*****

In CSM as in Colomoncagua, both women and men have found themselves doing new and different work. Brought up to be peasant farmers and housewives like their parents and generations before them, most of the Community's inhabitants could never have anticipated the range of jobs now on offer to them: administrative jobs, technical jobs, jobs as teachers, nurses, librarians, town planners, carpenters, bricklayers, motor mechanics, drivers, policemen, barbers, land surveyors, photographers, radio reporters, bank clerks, secretaries, accountants, managers.

Elena is a lab technician. Aged 28, with two small children and a war-wounded husband, she accompanied FMLN units as a paramedic in the early 1980s. She is relatively well-educated, having completed six grades at school near Osicala before the war. Now she sits at a big table in the Community's tiny pathology lab, her head bent intently over a gleaming microscope. Together with a Basque medical student who is working here for the summer, she is preparing slides from faeces for tests. From time to time she looks up to check what she sees against a chart showing various kinds of intestinal parasite.

The lab is a cubbyhole, partitioned off only a few weeks ago from the dentist's surgery next door, from which the whine of very old drills emanates. The three microscopes stand out from their far lower-tech surroundings: wooden shelves and stools on a beaten earth floor, a few boxes of chemical agents, one rack of test-tubes, tin trays for holding samples and slides. The specimens have arrived from all parts of the Community and other villages in the zone in pill-bottles or boxes, leaking plastic bags, or grubby twists of paper. But long Latinate names trip fluently off Elena's tongue as she describes the tests the lab can do: "leucocytes, haemoglobin, histolytic amoebae, gonococci, and then there's gynaecological and pregnancy testing".

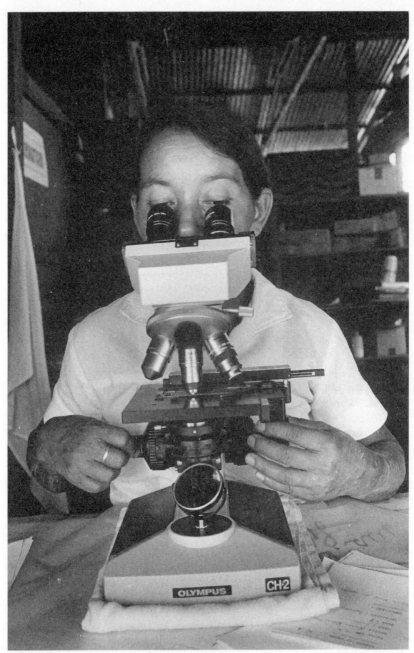

Lab technician. Women in the Community
are doing new and different work.

Jenny Matthews

Her confidence and skill are impressive, but Elena is very modest. "I've learned quite a bit on the practical side, but I know hardly any theory. I learned the techniques in Colomoncagua; but the training they gave us was very short, just a week or so. A Honduran lab technician taught me, and I also had some training from a French lab technician there. We had two laboratories in the camp." She is keen to develop her knowledge and skills further: "I'd like to get more training in this work, because really, I don't know anything about the theory. I'd really like to go to university."

Elena may inherit her thirst for knowledge from her mother Milagros, a respected and widely-read teacher. Her younger sister, Yanira, commutes to Perquín every day. She is working in an oral history centre, "collecting the life stories of people who've lived in Perquín, Arambala, and El Barrial, where the worst of the fighting was. We're going back twenty years, and the Centre will also be a kind of museum for those who are just growing up now and don't know anything about all that happened here."

*****

People who work for themselves, although far more numerous than those who work for the Community, have a much narrower range of job options. Many, like Cleotilde at Quebrachos, keep shops, and this is the largest and most rapidly growing group. Few of them, however, do as well as Cleotilde. There is dressmaking and tailoring: quite a number of people bought sewing machines sold off by the clothing factory. A few women still make a little money as midwives, a craft that has always existed alongside the Community's health service. Attempts to start up small private eating-places have not taken off, probably because only foreigners and visitors eat out. The list of loans made by the Bank show a growing number of people, some of them in groups, buying and breeding livestock for sale. But on the whole, subsistence agriculture in the *milpa* – or hired labour on other people's *milpa* – is the only option for those without Community jobs, especially since there is little if any training in the kind of skills people need to start up their own businesses.

At lunchtime, we meet Cipriano Sánchez. He lives with his second wife and their children in San Luis. Cipriano comes from Cacaopera in eastern Morazán, and was in the advance party that returned to El Salvador in November 1989 to prepare the way for the main repatriation. He has many years' experience, in Colomoncagua and before the flight, as a literacy teacher and lay preacher. But here he has no job with the

Community nor any independent business. He does not get the special food assistance for the elderly, as he is only 53. His own *milpa* does not yield even enough to support the family, and he has to buy extra maize. "How do you earn the money for that?" we ask.

"Well," Cipriano replies, "by working as a day-labourer. Sometimes you can earn ¢15 (about £1) a day without a meal, and if you get a meal it's ¢5. With that we can buy a few bushels of maize to survive on."

To earn the equivalent of a Community wage of ¢430 (about £28.60), he would have to work on someone else's land every day of the month.

*****

Payment of wages to the people working for the Community's various organisations, was approved by a General Assembly and introduced in January 1992. At first the wage was set at ¢20 a month, and then increased to 30, 40 and eventually to its present level of ¢430 to ¢700. Payment by piecework is being considered in some projects.

Darío Chicas, head of the Community's production division, CODEMO, explains how wages evolved::

"In the refugee camp there were no wages, no circulation, no money. Here in Ciudad Segundo Montes, we began working on the basis of a stipend or little incentives; but we soon came up against a problem: some people weren't involved in communal tasks since coming back, while others were; but both groups were getting assistance equally. So on the one hand you had people working communally, building houses, putting in water systems, getting production going, and working in health and education, while other people were getting on with buying their cows, pigs, hens and had started trading for themselves. And so you got an imbalance between the living standards of the communal workers and the individual ones, which wasn't really fair."

The leadership was worried that people who were sacrificing the chance to make a profit for the sake of the community endeavour – by far the most politically desirable option – might become disaffected if they saw themselves falling too far behind those who were not contributing to the communal project. Some Community employees were already becoming resentful and their efficiency and commitment were suffering.

There are several flaws in this argument, however. One is the assumption that all individuals are capable of making a profit, or indeed a living, or even of working at all. By no means all are as resourceful as traders like Cleotilde, have as good business sense, or possess an initial source of capital with which to launch a small business. In fact, the IDEA survey found that only 81 people in the Community had their own businesses. The only livelihood open to most private workers is subsistence level agriculture: the *milpa* and livestock – mostly limited to a few hens, half-a-dozen pigs, one or two cows.

The second problem is that subsistence agriculture, while it may sustain a family in terms of food – and many of the family plots at CSM are too small or too barren to do even that – does not generate the cash to buy other necessities, including those that would allow them to maintain their economic activity. Possibly one or two families have enough cows or pigs to make a small cash income; but hardly anyone has enough land, or good enough land, to be able to produce surplus crops for sale. So even if private workers have more time than the Community employees to work their own land, the activity brings them little or no money. It is this inability to earn money that puts them at a disadvantage compared with Community employees.

A third flaw is the assumption that working or not working for the Community is always a real choice, open to all. In fact there are nowhere near enough jobs in the Community's structures to give everyone employment and such jobs are decreasing in number as the aid funding which makes them possible comes to an end or is redirected. Only about a third of the economically active population – itself a slender 26.7 per cent of the total population, according to IDEA – is employed directly by the Community; and that percentage is falling as the Community grapples with the goal of self-sufficiency and profitability.

Already some workplaces have been closed and staff laid off, particularly in non-productive, service-providing sectors. The number of teachers has been cut and some of them have gone off to teach in other communities or repopulations or have been redeployed elsewhere in CSM. The opening hours of the clinics have been reduced. In Social Communication, the Community's culture and media organisation, the photography and video workshop has been forced to go part-time and the Community's newspaper ceased independent production in April 1992. There have been a few attempts to provide temporary employment but they are sporadic. Generating new employment is a concern widely voiced by citizens of CSM.

In fact the introduction of wages, while intended to close one potential wealth gap – between community and private workers – has created another – between the employed and the unemployed. To make matters worse, Community employees receive some subsidies not offered to individuals: for instance, they are entitled to pay a lower interest rate on loans from BANCOMO, the Community's bank; and they pay only half as much to enrol their pre-school children in the Community's day nurseries. The latter provision clearly discriminates against women, especially single mothers, many of whom are not employed by the Community. They have no chance of obtaining any other employment, unless their childcare problems are resolved.

On the whole, the Community's employees are perceived to be better off than most others. But even they do not always have enough to live on, especially if their families are large and there are only one or two breadwinners. According to the IDEA survey, many people in the Community feel that wages should be set at a minimum of ¢500 a month, because a family of seven would need at least ¢1,500 a month to make ends meet.

Luis is one of these people. From eight until four each day, he works in the Community's Urban Development organisation, as a surveyor. When he comes home, he puts in a few hours, until it is dark, making and mending clothes at the sewing machine he was able to buy when the Community reduced the size of its clothing factory. As well as this, Luis' wife runs a shop in the front room of their house. Luis says the family needs all three jobs, because the Community wage alone is not enough to support them. So how does a single mother with five small children and no living except her *milpa* and her sisal-spinning, survive?

The leadership of CSM intends the gradual rise of wages, in parallel with gradual reduction in aid, to be part of the strategy for reintegrating the repatriated Community into national economic life. The aim is to inject enough money into the Community economy to launch private, as well as communal commercial activity. But the Community's wages themselves are largely paid out of aid money, a finite source; and even these wages are not generally high enough for a family to live on.

The hard fact is that CSM is extremely poor. Yet it is the richest place in northern Morazán. A few days later we are hitching a ride up to Quebrachos in a pick-up truck belonging to one of the timber companies in Perquín. "Where are you going?" asks one of the men riding in the back of the truck.

"Just here: we're staying in Ciudad Segundo Montes."

"Ah, Ciudad Segundo Montes," he replies, "*allí corre mucho pisto, ¿no?*" [loads of money there, eh?]

*****

Whether or not they do any waged work, virtually every family in the Community cultivates its plot of land. Community employees go to the *milpa* before and after the eight-hour working day. Reconciling the demands and work rhythms of an agricultural livelihood with those of urban life and semi-industrial production has proved difficult. Apart from the adverse effect on productivity of doing several hours' work in the *milpa* as well as their Community workday, people tend to stay away from their jobs at harvest or sowing time. This is natural, says Blanca Hernández, a planner and administrator at CODEMO:

> "It's the custom to grow maize for food and people don't regard other work as so secure, even though it's earning them money ... They have this idea that maize is the only thing they can rely on. We always come up against this obstacle in the harvest season, even though we ask them to try harder at work."

*****

Isabel works in one of the CODEMO enterprises earmarked for decentralisation, or for 'handing over to the workers', as people tend to call it. She sells handicrafts made in the Community's workshops in one of the row of small shops by the San Luis bus-stop. For a time, she thinks, she will go on getting a wage from CODEMO, and will pay rent for the premises but be compensated for this with a percentage of what she sells. But later, her wage will cease, and then she will get only the earnings from her sales and will have to pay her rent out of that.

Isabel's main worry is that her shop depends heavily on tourism. It is full of decorative objects – ornate fringed sheaths for machetes, embroidered tablecloths and handkerchiefs, painted cups and vases – that Community residents are not very likely to buy regularly. "Last month, when there were lots of visitors, I sold a lot; but if there are fewer visitors this month I'll earn less." She is also not very sure whether the Community workshops will continue to sell their produce at the same prices to the shops once they are privatised. "We just don't know what degree of control CODEMO will have over the shops."

Community leaders insist that workers will be consulted and assisted with the privatisation of their enterprises, and that agreements with workers will be sought in each case. According to Juan José, "we're aware that if we really want the shops to take off, we'll have to support them in some way, with some kind of technical assistance and publicity."

Many workers, however, are either confused about how the 'handing over' process will work in practice or alarmed at what they see as abandonment. Isabel is not clear what proportion of her sales she will be able to keep as her salary once her shop is handed over to her. When we ask Ana and Marina, on the Copinolar building site, whether there are meetings of the workers on the site with the leaders of Urban Development to discuss progress, Ana hedges. "A bit," she says cautiously. "Not really about the work, though. They don't know how to get people together; it only happens when something goes wrong." Marina chimes in: "We're behind in that respect, I think, because there's no attempt to get people to meet, motivate them, nothing like that. Our work area's making a mistake in not attending to that kind of thing."

We see this frustration all too frequently. Many workers feel ill-informed and powerless. Leaders seem not to have realised that excluding the workers from decision-making simply reinforces their passivity, the very quality they are hoping to overcome by promoting individual initiative.

The results of the teachers' assembly give some indication of what Community employees think about work and employment. The views of those not employed by the Community are far harder to gauge, for they have no equivalent forum. There is a growing feeling that the Community is beginning to divide into two distinct public and private sectors. Most people agree in principle with the need for private economic initiatives, but are concerned about the shortage of jobs – meaning jobs paid for by the Community. Few people have the confidence or the capital to start up or run a business.

In the meantime, the Community's employees are being seen, increasingly, as an elite, the fortunate few who enjoy job security, assured wages, and subsidies. When the April 1992 General Assembly voted, after hot debate, to award the first batch of permanent houses to Community workers still living in provisional housing, rather than to single mothers, the decision prompted remarks that those who were already relatively well off were being further favoured. Diplomatically, the Community leadership backed down and added single mothers with large families to the list of those qualifying for new housing. But there have even been rumours that some people in administrative positions are reserving jobs for members of their families. Even if they are untrue, such views are divisive and damaging to the Community as a whole.

19
The Nursery

Towards the end of the afternoon, we meet Marina again. She has come to fetch her four-month-old baby from the nursery in San Luis. This nursery is a jollier place than the drowsy barn at El Barrial. Its walls are brightened with some pictures and alphabet charts, and although there aren't many toys, nursery staff are playing games with the children. As we enter, a young woman is directing a group of three-year-olds as they dance barefoot in a circle and sing a song to end the day.

About 45 children are at the nursery today, including the four- and five-year-olds from the kindergarten class who join the nursery group for the afternoon. However, María, the nursery supervisor remarks that this is less than half the highest attendance the nursery has seen and well below its regular numbers. Why has attendance fallen so sharply? Because, says María, the fees have gone up. At first, she explains, the nursery was a free service and a hundred children attended. But, in line with the new drive for every area of the Community to become self-sufficient, the executive committee decided to charge a fee of ¢50 (about 3.5p) per child per day from July 1992. Several mothers stopped bringing their children immediately. Now, in early September, the fee has just doubled, prompting a further drop in nursery attendance. "And it'll keep on falling," María warns, "if people's wages don't go up." All the staff at the San Luis nursery believe strongly in the need for the nurseries as a social service and think it is only the cost that keeps people from using them to the full.

CSM now has over 800 single mothers with an average of three or four children each. Where so many women are the sole breadwinners in their households, some kind of socialised childcare is crucial. Community nurseries for the under-fives were set up in Colomoncagua in the mid-eighties, almost certainly at the suggestion of international volunteers, for whom socialised childcare would have been seen as indispensable if women were to play an active role in the life of the Community. The nurseries began as informal arrangements where older women kept an eye on the smallest children during working hours. As funding was obtained, the nurseries became institutionalised, and they were started up again after repatriation more or less as a matter of course. There is one in each settlement. As we have seen, their quality and atmosphere vary considerably and depend on the energy and imagination of the women – and they are all women – who staff them. They work the normal CSM day, from 8am to 4pm. The children get something to eat at around 11 o'clock: fruit or salad vegetables, milk, sometimes a bowl of soup with meat in it. Mothers can send their babies to the nursery from as young as two months.

In practice, however, only the Community employees use the nurseries; and in fact, for women with a Community wage at its present level, ¢50-60 (up to £4) a month for nursery fees is perhaps not so crippling as María suggests. It is the women without Community jobs who really can't afford the nurseries – not only because they usually earn less than a Community wage but also because they have to pay more for the nursery. A foreign worker who is training women in nursery education explains:

"People working in Community projects pay ¢1 for the nursery, while others pay ¢2. So people who aren't working for the Community are discriminated against. You could say, that's because they've got lots of *milpa*, lots of other work. But there are lots of people who can't find work ... People are told, if you want to work for yourself, you must pay to put your child in the nursery."

*****

The nurseries have proved to be eminently fundable, popular with development agencies and solidarity groups alike. They are unlikely to disappear as long as agencies continue to like them and fund them; and they do provide a healthy number of Community jobs. There are currently twenty women working in the San Luis nursery alone, and six or seven more in its kitchen, plus a supervisor and three cleaners – an extremely high infant/carer ratio if there are only thirty to forty children attending.

But the existence of the nurseries does not necessarily mean that the Community leadership is politically committed to making it possible for women to earn a living, especially outside the Community's own public sector. It is certainly recognised that many areas of work would have no workforce without socialised childcare; but the effective exclusion of private workers from using the nurseries reinforces a notion that the nurseries are there to assist the smooth running of Community structures rather than to give female breadwinners the chance of a livelihood.

Nor has the presence of the nurseries led to any lasting change in perceptions of childcare or the role of women. The foreign nursery education trainer feels that working in a nursery is not seen as a skilled job requiring training but simply as a 'natural' occupation for women, an extension of looking after small children at home. This attitude was revealed recently when the leadership began laying off nursery workers for two-month periods so that they could offer two months' work in the nurseries to unemployed single mothers. The foreign worker argues that this negates the training in nursery education she is employed to give and that, well-intentioned as it is, the measure is based on a view of work with young children as essentially unskilled.

It also raises the question of whether the nurseries are thought of as educative or simply as a social service. Formally, they are part of the remit of Communal Services. Some people think the main purpose of the nurseries is to provide free food. Their educational value is not universally recognised in the Community.

The nurseries could be a valuable investment in CSM's development, as a service enabling women to earn a living, as a source of skilled employment, and in the long term as an important early learning experience. But at present they are a poignant example of the dilemmas the Community is facing as it strives to become economically self-sufficient but at the same time tries to preserve community values and meet the expectations of a population alert to any erosion of the social benefits they have been used to.

*****

The nursery issue also illustrates the familiar tendency to provide women with childcare facilities in wartime when they are needed to replace a male workforce, and then to curtail them as a 'luxury' as soon as the war is over. The nurseries do not come cheap, and the nursery education trainer is worried that they may be sacrificed in favour of other projects such as employing the ex-combatants and war-wounded.

In fact, women's high level of employment in CSM is coming under threat on a number of fronts. Blanca Hernández worked as a health promoter with pregnant women and as a metalwork solderer before her present job as an administrator in CODEMO. She feels that women's incorporation into productive work outside the home is not as high as it was in Colomoncagua:

"A lot of the work here is heavier and more demanding. It's not like the refuge where you worked voluntarily. Here, women haven't been able to do as much of the heavier work as men: for instance, the

San Luis nursery

Jenny Matthews

vehicle workshop had women in it at the start, but not anymore. There are two women in metalwork, because they have special skills... Now we're looking for other areas to provide new jobs for women: small livestock, tailoring, pottery, sisal products, leatherwork."

There seems to be a danger of restricting women's employment to 'feminine' jobs like handicrafts. With the return to El Salvador and a partial return to traditional agricultural livelihoods, many traditional ideas about women's role and women's place have come creeping back, not only among men but among some women themselves. As Rosa Elia points out:

"Back in Colomoncagua, everything was provided for us. Now it's all changed. Here, if a woman doesn't have work, she looks for a man to keep her! And sometimes this backfires, because the men are irresponsible and all they do is leave her with another child and go off somewhere else."

This general reassertion of male dominance in the Community – and the challenge to women's jobs – will inevitably increase when the combatants, who are mostly male, return to civilian life. CSM expects to receive about a thousand ex-combatants.

The problem, familiar to all societies emerging from war, is compounded here by the fact that communities who sympathised with the FMLN during the war feel they have a responsibility to its members now the war is over. It is universally agreed that the demobilised and the war-wounded deserve to be rewarded with employment. At a more pragmatic level, the presence of several hundred disgruntled young men without work could have a highly destabilising and troublesome influence on the community. But it is the women in the community who will have to stand aside, not men.

"I think it's like what people have told me about the Second World War," says Rosa Elia; "women had a big role during the war, but afterwards they returned to the home and lost everything they'd gained."

*****

Some women insist, however, that there is no going back, and that their right to work must be defended. So on Sunday morning we are up with the sparrows to attend, at 7am, the first meeting of the coordinating committee of a new women's organisation, which has been named the Association for the Integral Development of Women, ADIM. The Association's purpose is precisely to create and safeguard work opportunities and sources of income-generation specifically for women. It is only a week old, having been formed at a public meeting attended by 140 women the previous Sunday which elected this group to coordinate it.

Seven women are here today. All seven work with the Community and all already have many commitments. Mabel is the head of Social Communications; Martina works in Communal Services; Lorenza is active in pastoral work and the Christian Mothers' Committee; Tania is responsible for the nurseries at community level. Two other women have already resigned from the committee for lack of time to take on another commitment. "It's the same old contradiction," Lorenza says. "No one has any time, but at the same time everyone knows that solving women's economic problems is also important." Everyone agrees, ruefully.

We meet in the open air, on the steep slope behind the offices of Social Communication. We sit on tree roots and big stones. The mood is not optimistic. The discussion concentrates less on what the organisation will do than on whether it will be possible to do anything. Lorenza raises a difficult problem. "We'll have to explain very clearly that this isn't a job creation programme for women who already have jobs, and that women in ADIM aren't being paid anything." Already there seem to have been signs of resentment from women without Community jobs who think the women's organisation is a kind of 'jobs-for-the-girls' club. "Yes," says Mabel, "it's very important to get the idea across that this organisation is for all women."

Finally, we get to the practical issue of income-generating projects for women. Lorenza reports that the Community's Office of Social Welfare is looking at the question of women who have no work and many children. They are considering collective projects producing things like bread, ice-cream, or hammocks. But ADIM should cast its net wider, she adds, and address all women in the Community.

Several women in the group make other suggestions for projects, mostly involving food production of one kind or another. They discuss the need to educate women about the kind of commitment necessary to keep income-generating projects going: an earlier women's project failed because the women who took part in it couldn't agree on the principle of ploughing half their profits back into the project. This leads to a longer discussion about wages and how much people could expect to be paid for what quantity or quality of work.

Towards the end of the meeting, Mabel raises the question of promoting women's leadership, which should be an objective of ADIM as important as promoting income-generating projects. "If we don't pay attention to that, the Community will end up being run entirely by men," she warns. ADIM is very new and fragile. There is no time. There is no funding except for a calf promised by the cattle project which the women can sell or raffle. The organisation needs technical advice. And, although women are an overwhelming majority of the workforce and are relatively well represented at organising and administrative levels in the Community, only a small number of them have a clear perception of women's gender interests. As Mabel remarks wryly, "Women are incorporated – but they're certainly not organised!"

20
Pastoral

L orenzo López – Lencho – lives at the northern end of San Luis, in a newish house made of fibre-board and roofed with corrugated iron. Lencho is one of the Community's senior and most respected catechists or lay preachers and he has invited us to meet some people involved in pastoral work at CSM, among them his neighbour, Juana Orellana. They are all people in their fifties or sixties, soft-voiced and gentle in manner. We sit in the doorway of the little house, for San Luis is stifled under the blanket of motionless heat that always precedes a big storm here. Tall clouds, ice-cream shading to gunmetal, are massing overhead like heavy cavalry.

The religious teaching and forms of worship engaged in at CSM are based on the teachings of liberation theology, and have their roots in the work done by priests and nuns with poor communities in the late 1960s and early 1970s. It uses stories from the Bible to lead people to discover parallels with their own lives and understand the true reasons for their poverty.

"That was our real crime, you know, to study the Bible and tell the truth," Juana says. "The Bible says that a person has to act in order to be free – but we didn't know it would lead to terror and war!"

Both Lencho and Juana experienced at first hand the excitement, and the danger, of the new ideas reaching isolated hamlets that seldom saw a priest. It started in 1970, Lencho tells us:

"The catechists invited people from the hamlets to religious centres like El Castaño [in Chalatenango, opened in 1968 by priests from Cleveland, Ohio], where we did some training, some Bible study, and some work on motivating people.

"We began to reflect on the Bible. It was great, because we'd never had a priest – he only came round on special feast days. You had to pay to have a Mass said, for instance for someone who'd died: it was ¢10-15 per Mass! The only place that had regular Sunday Mass was Jocoaitique, where the priest was based. So we'd get together for a Celebration of the Word [liturgy] with all the hamlets in the area, choosing a text everyone knew.

And we began to realise that God didn't make things just for some people, but that the land was for everyone. We saw this very clearly from our reading, we studied it well. We discovered that we weren't poor because God wanted us to be poor, as we'd always thought. Through the Bible we discovered that God created everything for everybody - and if that was so, how was it that only some of the people had rights? How was it that the rich could eat, but the poor could only watch and weep and endure?

So those of us who'd been meeting began to organise and to discuss what we could do. Some people with little plots of land said they were prepared to make them into a communal *milpa*. We took half an acre of land to make a common field for the whole village. It wasn't much, but it really raised people's morale. We shared it all out family by family. But making this communal *milpa* brought the repression down on us. Our crime was to give – because the rich never give anything away, so they don't like seeing other people doing it."

"At the time," Juana adds, "when the catechists were holding meetings and talks and giving people guidance, we weren't afraid. We never thought these activities would give us cause for fear."

Lencho recalls one of the collective efforts his community made:

"There was this young man who was very poor. He lived on his own, and one day another lad burnt his house down after a quarrel and left him with nothing. The men got together and decided to help him out. Each man brought a plank and 25 men worked hard to build him another house, fast. We got him a bed, a table, and some chairs, too, because he'd lost everything. It wasn't easy to convince everyone, mind you, but it's not enough just to go to meetings and talk, you have to put it into practice. And if we poor people don't help ourselves, who else will? So we all gave something: those who had more gave more, and those who had less gave less; and those who had nothing brought their will to be with us, to accompany us.

But all this was threatening to the rich. They didn't like us doing collective work, and talking about land being for everyone, not just for them. They began to call us subversives – that was the new word we began to hear. Then the first catechists were persecuted. I wasn't a catechist at that time. I just went along and listened and learned ..."

In fact, Lencho had to play a double game, for he was in the local militia and had to hide his links with the catechists. "They told us to watch these groups that were holding meetings and see what they did." As the system of informers was instituted, things became even more dangerous. "I knew

I was gambling with my life; but many people lived this way, hiding what they were doing. They were the first to die."

*****

Many of those who fled to Honduras took their faith and their way of living it with them. Pastoral work was organised early on at Colomoncagua. It was a continuation of the work begun in El Salvador, even though, as Tacho from El Barrial reminds us, "nearly all the catechists who had awakened the spirit of the communities in Morazán were killed". Eventually there were 660 'delegates of the word' (lay preachers) at Colomoncagua. Lencho became a catechist in the refugee camp, as did Juana:

"I wasn't really familiar with the Bible, I'd never held a Bible in my hands – oh, I'd listened to readings, I liked that, but no one would lend me a Bible to read. So it was in the refuge that I learnt a bit about working with people; there were some nuns who helped us study the Bible."

Angel Romero, a silver-haired, grey-eyed man who is in charge of the education supplies store, was a lay preacher at Colomoncagua. He talks of the way the pastoral work was organised:

"We gave catechesis twice a week to adults and children, held 'Celebrations of the Word' and visited the sub-camps, keeping people's spirits up. We'd have readings, then hold discussions and reflections on the meaning of the passage we'd read in terms of the life of the community. We taught that not only we, but others before us had suffered too, and it was written down, how there had to be sufferings and migrations. We compared our experience with the Flight into Egypt, and how Moses had led the people across the Red Sea. It was a job that required lots of commitment, time, and meetings."

Like so many of the activities in Colomoncagua, pastoral work was therapeutic and morale-raising, as Juana implies:

"The biblical texts gave us the strength to go on, spiritual strength. And they also taught the respect that people ought to have for each other as human beings."

*****

Just as they compare their crossing into Honduras with the biblical flight into Egypt, the pastoral workers describe their return in terms of a resurrection and biblical imagery permeates the language they use about the Community now. The idea of solidarity is illustrated by the parable of the Good Samaritan, and reconciliation in passages such as this from the Old Testament:

The wolf also shall dwell with the lamb, and the leopard shall lie down with the kid; and the calf and the young lion and the fatling together – and the cow and the bear shall feed; their young ones shall lie down together; and the lion shall eat straw like the ox. (Isaiah 11:6-9)

The nuts and bolts of pastoral work in CSM are much the same as they were in Colomoncagua: catechesis meetings on Wednesdays, Mass or a Celebration of the Word on Sundays. Many women are members of the Congregation of Christian Mothers, a direct descendant of the mothers' committees in the refuge, and reflection groups for men are being set up, Tacho tells us, "since men have had less opportunity in this respect than women, because of their work".

Isn't it harder to keep track of people, with the community here so much more widely scattered than it was in Colomoncagua?

"Not really," says Lencho.

"Now that we're not divided up into camps and sub-camps, the catechists and lay preachers each look after a group of people. Each group has its topic; the catechists inform their groups in advance and tell them to bring their ideas. They also let people know when the priest is coming and things like that."

Nonetheless, the number of people involved in religious activity has fallen noticeably since the return, and pastoral work is becoming increasingly the preserve of older members of the Community. The catechists are anxious to find ways of keeping the numbers up and of attracting young people. It's not so easy, Lencho admits, "especially now that we have extra responsibilities – we all have our work, we have our families to support as well. Life's much more complex now."

Fr Rogelio, on the other hand, sees no reason for pessimism.

"At Colomoncagua, the only entertainment on Sundays was to go to Mass; now there are dozens of things to do. The catechists feel they're losing their grip. But I think they're worrying too much. I keep saying to them, 'Forget Colomoncagua; we're in Ciudad Segundo Montes now, back to normal life.' They'll say, 'We had a reflexion, but it was

Mass with Fr Rogelio

Jenny Matthews

useless.' 'Why? How many people turned up?' 'Fifty.' 'Good Lord,' I say to them, 'where else would you get fifty people to come to a service?'"

Rogelio also feels it may be time to modify the collectivist thrust of the teaching, particularly since the Community is now open to influence from evangelical Protestant groups:

"It's hard to get across to people the difference between us and those groups. They try to ignore social commitment, they preach a Christianity which never gets beyond the personal and the family sphere. But they do offer something that people might not find in our pastoral vision ... Our pastoral work has been very committed. During the war we could never preach without reminding people of the task, the struggle, alongside the people ... It was all 'the people': 'unite with the people', 'struggle beside the people'. In this new situation, I think we're feeling the need to broaden out our focus and include not just social commitment, but people's commitment to their family, their community, and their personal lives."

It is understandably hard, however, for people whose lives were directly touched by the exhilarating religious experience of the 1970s to return to a more individualistic view without some qualms. The discovery that people are stronger together than separately transformed many lives and fuelled a fierce commitment to the collective ideal – an ideal, moreover, for which many people struggled and died. Older members of the community have very clear memories of this region as it was before the war: a land of little farms and hamlets, of maguey plantations marching across the still-wooded mountainsides, of saints' day processions and traditional dances going back to pre-Columbian times; but they also remember the ceaseless toil, the brutally unequal wealth distribution, and the petty tyrannies of authority figures – the local government officials, the judges, the policemen and soldiers, the city-bred schoolteachers for whom poor, isolated Morazán was a hardship posting, 'the Siberia of El Salvador'. For people like Lencho and Juana, organising their lives 'in community' was first a revelation and then a cause for bitter sacrifice, and they are dismayed at the prospect of the dilution of communal values:

"It's not a house we're building now, it's peace. We've succeeded in building peace through the force of unity ... we've lived together and learned to work together, and although we aren't working like that now, we've discovered that unity is strength. And the same goes for building the peace: for if we split off from each other and each start to live apart from the rest, people aren't going to have contact with each other, and we'll forget what happened before, we'll forget the great commitment we had to peace, and we won't finish what we started."

*****

With so many of the lay preachers in Ciudad Segundo Montes coming from the over-50 age group, it is natural that they should be leaders and representatives of the older section of the Community, some of the hardest hit by the economic changes set in motion by the Peace Accords.

Nemesio Carrillo is 81. He's lived through two world wars and two wars in his own country: the Football War with Honduras, and the civil war just ending. He's been a small landowner and cattle-farmer. Though his parents were landless, by the late 1970s he owned over fifty head of cattle and employed half a dozen labourers. He's had two wives, and many children. But as he talks to us, perched on a sack of maize in a shadow-filled corner of his two-room clapboard house, growing old here doesn't seem like the well-earned homecoming of a long life so much as a poor bargain, the only thing on offer.

"It's all different now. There's more freedom here; but we're still as poor as ever. Poverty's not something you can cure overnight. It'll take a long time. I've got a place I could live in down in Torola. But how can I leave here now? Perhaps I'll die here, perhaps this is where death will catch up with me."

Although CSM is often called 'a community of children and old people', its 619 people aged over sixty represent less than ten per cent of the population. According to the IDEA census, over three-quarters of them – 485 people, including eleven people over 85 – are still working, half of these as housewives. Several people we have talked to, however, suggest that there is a retirement age for Community employees. José María, whom we met at El Barrial, says that "people participate up to a certain age, but once we're over sixty, there's hardly any work for us. They say it's better for the young people to have the jobs." Rafaela the potter, too, has been told she is too old for Community work.

Looking after elderly people is seen as a natural function of the family, and the Community has no special policies or provisions for elderly people except for a limited programme of food distribution – all that is left of the food aid the whole community received until the end of 1991. Opinions of the efficacy and availability of the food distribution vary widely. José María says it is available but not very generous: "just tortillas and a few beans; sometimes there isn't any and we don't get anything;" so they cannot afford to retire from the *milpa*. But according to another elderly man, Román, not all elderly people qualify for food aid, inclusion on the list depending on the quantity of maize you can grow for yourself.

There are no special housing arrangements for elderly people, such as priority access to the newly-built permanent housing, nor any socialised support for those living alone, like Rafaela, or without a strong family support system. Román, for instance, has to depend on his surviving daughter who lives next door to him and cooks for him. His family is tragically fragmented. His other daughter was killed, he tells us, just for being his daughter, because he was known to be an active catechist close to Fr Miguel Ventura. One of his sons died fighting in the war and the rest of the family escaped to safety to Sonsonate, a town in western El Salvador relatively untouched by fighting; they now see no reason to return to poverty in Morazán. "I know I won't see any big changes in my lifetime," Román says sadly, "but I've struggled all my life so that things will be different for my children."

21
The Capital

"I'm not from the Community, you know," says Julio. "I come from Santa Ana in the west. I used to have my own vehicle and work for people in Colonia Escalón in San Salvador. That's where all the rich people live who are exploiting this country. My boss was one of the founders of ARENA. He's an ex-Foreign Minister and he's travelled all over. He owns orange and coffee plantations, fruit and vegetable farms.

"I didn't like it much, seeing the things rich people do. During the 1989 offensive I was working in a house there, maintaining six vehicles, and I couldn't get to work because of the fighting. I asked my boss for time off until the fighting was over. When he paid me at the end of the month, he docked my pay for those three days."

Julio spits out of the pickup window, contemptuously. He is one of the regulars at the Cultural Centre cafeteria, usually to be seen laughing loudly and chatting with foreign visitors. Today, he is driving down to San Salvador to pick up a consignment of leather for the shoe factory, and we have seized the chance for a lift. We ask him what brought him to Ciudad Segundo Montes. He frowns, choosing his words carefully.

"I had a friend up here and I told him how fed up I was. He said there was work here in the Community – not a permanent job, but casual work. That was fine by me. I've felt really happy here. It's totally different to being in San Salvador or Santa Ana. I'm really impressed by the people here. You get to think that because you've been to university you know everything. But here I've learned a lot about how to live and how to care about others." Julio leans forward, concentrating on the road, as we come out of the hill country and enter San Francisco Gotera, the departmental capital of Morazán.

*****

Gotera is hot, smelly and shabby, but cheerful. It is emerging from over a decade as a garrison town and the relief is almost tangible. Throughout the war it has been the base for DM4, the army's Fourth Division, and one of the most important posts in the country, responsible for holding the line against the FMLN in northern Morazán. With the fighting over and the roadblocks dismantled, there is little to do for the soldiers confined to the massive barracks, the town's most salient feature. This accounts for the large number of well-muscled young men in new vests and running shorts cycling or jogging along the roads or playing football on the now-quiet airfield outside the town.

Close to the barracks, in the centre of the town, is the convent of the Sisters of St Clare, a cool haven of creamy tiles and green gardens after the stuffy heat and bustle of the streets. If you stay there overnight, you will be woken at 5am by a tuneless rendition of the Salvadorean National Anthem followed by the hoarse *"Un, dos, tres, cuat' ! Un, dos, tres, cuat'!"* of a drill sergeant. During the twelve years of war, the nuns have been woken many times by far more terrible evidence of army activity. Desperate people, sometimes badly injured, regularly found their way here, seeking food and shelter, denouncing army attacks and atrocities.

Sister Anselm arrived in San Francisco Gotera twenty years ago, just as the first catechists were being trained in El Salvador. In the old communities of San Luis, Quebrachos, El Mozote, Torola, people were using Bible study to interpret their own situation and improve it. "The people began to think," Sister Anselm recalls, "and there is nothing more dangerous."

It was an exhilarating moment, soon to be followed by years of repression that made pastoral work dangerous if not impossible. The army's notorious slogan, 'be a patriot – kill a priest', extended to catechists and lay preachers. Many of the catechists Anselm knew in the 1970s were killed by the army or death squads. Others went north into the mountains and joined the FMLN. Those who survived the war, and others returning from exile abroad, have begun to return to their villages. In May this year (1992), Anselm tells us, they had a reunion of more than 300 catechists of the parish at the pastoral centre in Gotera. Many were seeing friends, or even learning that they were still alive, for the first time in twelve years.

The Gotera parish team, consisting of Salvadorean and foreign religious people and nurses from the US Mennonite Central Committee, found their work in the early 1980s reduced to humanitarian assistance, carried out in conditions of extreme danger. They organised food distribution for the tidal waves of displaced people arriving in Gotera in the wake of the massacres of 1980 and 1981. Later in the decade they were able to quietly resume pastoral work; throughout the war they kept a register of human rights abuses reported to them by local people and often negotiated the release of prisoners with their neighbour, the Colonel in charge of DM4.

Now the parish is returning to normal life again. A pastoral centre has been opened, with meeting rooms, a space for worship and cultural presentations, a kitchen. The nuns' house always seems full of busy people – a young musical group rehearsing, a women's study group, as well as the steady stream of poor people seeking food, clothes, money, advice, comfort. Once a week, María Julia, who heads *Tutela Legal*, the Catholic Church's human rights organisation in San Salvador, passes through, very early in the morning. She is on her way to El Mozote to interview witnesses and to rendezvous with the judge appointed to investigate the massacre.

Gotera is a different world from CSM. Miguel, a young man who drives the JCB truck at CSM, is probably the only Community employee who lives in the town. Originally from San Miguel, he dresses in an American-style lumberjack shirt and speaks a little English. One day his 11-year-old son picked up a bomb left lying around by soldiers. It exploded, severing his hand. The army did nothing for them. Miguel sold two vehicles to raise the US$5,000 for an artificial arm, which was fitted in Boston after a US organisation paid their fares to the USA. Miguel says people in Gotera give him funny looks for working at CSM, for they still think of the Community as a nest of guerrillas, even though many small traders now regularly do business in the Community at marketplaces and shops. Nevertheless, attitudes are slowly changing. There is still a lot of distrust, if not open hostility, but also great curiosity and some approval. The opening up of the region and the trading links with the Community have already made it seem less strange and dangerous.

*****

From Gotera we take the road to San Miguel, which we skirt before heading south-west into Usulután. Julio has chosen to head for the capital via the coast road. We pass through some of the most fertile farm land in the country: irrigated fields of maize and rice, roadside markets dwarfed by mountains of watermelon. We pass close to San Salvador's ugly international airport, before turning inland along the country's only motorway.

Like many capitals, San Salvador is two cities, divided by money. Its eastern end, around the old centre, is overcrowded and run down. To the north are the poor parishes of Mejicanos and Zacamil, where Christian base communities have been strong since the 1970s. The south and south-west of the city are where the really rich live, sheltered behind high electrified fences while armed guards lounge at the gates, chatting up the maidservants and street vendors.

Behind the great riches, great poverty. Wander just a few yards off the unnaturally tranquil, landscaped crescents of opulent Escalón, or the streets of respectable Miramonte ('Hillview') or Lomas de Versalles ('Versailles Heights'), and you will come upon steep, weedy ravines. Tumble-down shacks are strewn down their flanks among the undergrowth, like garbage dumped over the edge. They look as though the next gust of wind might sweep them away, and the heavy rains of June and September often do. Here, in the interstices of prosperity, is where many of the war-displaced have found a fragile refuge.

In the capital, security is much more on people's minds than in Morazán. Ironically, as the dangers of war recede, sharply rising crime is making San Salvador a more dangerous city than ever before. Muggings at gunpoint and bus holdups are commonplace. The FMLN blames demobilised government soldiers, security men, and their hangers-on, and even hints at the deliberate creation of an atmosphere of uncertainty to justify the retention of the old security forces.

CSM has its own office in San Salvador, in a moderately well-heeled middle-class suburb: not in the electric-fence-and-armed-guard league, but one where the houses are comfortable and the cars large, plentiful, and mostly parked on the footpath. Several non-governmental organisations (NGOs), church organisations and development agencies have their offices in this neighbourhood, while the human rights organisation Americas Watch and the FMLN's Reconstruction Office are nearby.

Many other international and Salvadorean NGOs are dotted about the city, some of them long-established, others part of a more recent influx of international interest and a proliferation of new national NGOs of all political stripes as the war approached its end.

In the office, we find several meetings going on. Someone is giving an interview to a journalist who hasn't time to go out to the Community. A small group is poring over specifications for the new housing. A volunteer is giving one of the staff a lesson in computing. Upstairs, the secretarial pool is busy at clattering manual typewriters or queuing for the photocopier. Most of them are city women; none is from the Community.

The office is largely run by foreign and Salvadorean technical people but has a member of the Community's *Junta Directiva* on the staff as well. Concha spends the working week in San Salvador and comes home each weekend to her family in Meanguera village. The office's chief job is to manage the flow of aid money, elaborating project proposals, preparing reports for funders, and buying large capital goods such as machinery; but it also serves as a first point of reference for visitors to CSM.

*****

Only a few blocks away from the office is FASTRAS, where we are meeting with people from organisations that support the Community. FASTRAS (Salvadorean Workers' Foundation for Self-Management and Solidarity) was founded in 1986 to provide technical, organisational, and fundraising support to organisations and communities in eastern El Salvador. It played a key role in facilitating the repatriation and mediating the Community's early funding proposals to international donors such as the European Community and European NGOs. Now it works with Segundo Montes in a wider context, as Jaime, one of its staff, explains:

"We see Ciudad Segundo Montes within a global view of the eastern zone, of which Morazán is a part. It's obviously impossible to have one big group of people in the zone who are more qualified and better resourced than the rest; it leads to uneven development."

Silvia is from a Central American organisation which works with refugees and returnees. She points out that repatriated communities in fact represent only a small fraction of Salvadorean society: "There are about 30,000 returnees; so the repatriated communities are only a subculture of the Salvadorean population, and we can't apply their case to the rest of the country. But people from outside tend to concentrate on this particular case and get the impression that El Salvador consists of a series of super-organised, super-articulate communities with a much bigger vision of the world. The other communities in Morazán linked to PADECOMSM are much closer to the norm: they represent a truly Salvadorean form of organisation that sprang out of the most horrendous conditions, a tiny light kindled by the civilian population. PADECOMSM has a great deal to offer but we have to admit that it doesn't have the brilliance of Ciudad Segundo Montes."

"Haven't we aid donors ourselves created this disparity?" asks Patrick, the Canadian visitor. "We've given so much money to this community, both as refugees and returnees, that it's become a showpiece project."

"There are people who criticise Ciudad Segundo Montes for the amount of aid it has attracted," Jaime replies; "but we see this as a sector especially hard hit by the war, a population with many old people and mothers with children. These are vulnerable people and not the most ideal productive force."

"But these vulnerable people, as a community, have become the strongest and most confident social force in Morazán today," Patrick insists. "And what they've become most adept at is getting more funding."

"There's a reason for that," says Silvia. "It's as though the people who went to Colomoncagua had a kind of scholarship which enabled them to study for eight years; their universe became much wider because of all the international attention and the delegations; while the PADECOMSM people led a more ordinary life, they stayed the same, they stayed put, in their tiny universe, with a very limited capacity."

"But you can't say the PADECOMSM communities are not organised," Jaime stresses. "Their organisation just takes other forms. It's not directed so intensely towards external support."

"Yes, but this inequality in funding becomes self-perpetuating," says Anna, a foreign worker at CSM. "The PADECOMSM communities are underfunded precisely because they have a lower profile. So they stay low-profile and attract less funding. Agencies have got to recognise this and change their policy."

"We are starting to change," says Jean, a visitor from an aid agency. "many agencies now have joint projects with PADECOMSM and Ciudad Segundo Montes. But it's been very difficult to design projects without CSM taking a leading role. In their own project proposals Segundo Montes often describe PADECOMSM communities as beneficiaries rather than colleagues, consumers of what Segundo Montes produces."

But why has Segundo Montes been so favoured with aid? Is it just because of its high vulnerability? Were the communities that stayed in Morazán throughout the war not equally vulnerable?

Silvia says, "I've heard grumbles that the international community privileges the returnees because they correspond most closely to our interests and priorities: they're on our wavelength, they fit in very well with our needs as donors. And we do get things from CSM that we don't get from PADECOMSM – written proposals, reviews, discussions. The people at Ciudad Segundo Montes are at an entirely different level. In comparison, the people in PADECOMSM are less exciting to talk to, more timid and introvert, and it takes a very long time to get to know them."

"But we've been able to do more with less money in PADECOMSM communities," says Jean, "because projects in Segundo Montes are high-cost and our grants go towards maintaining infrastructure, whereas PADE-

COMSM projects are based more on providing credit for productive activities and health and education services."

Patrick thinks the presence of foreign workers, carried over from Colomoncagua to CSM, has a lot to answer for. "Many of the international volunteers accompanied the repatriation and still have a very strong influence on the Community. I think the internationals were necessary in the war for security purposes as much as anything else, but now the Community needs to break free of them and channel its energies towards more ordinary economic activities; learning how to market its produce, what to produce for the local market, for example."

But that means training, doesn't it? Wouldn't that be the most appropriate role for aid and technical assistance now? In administration, management and business skills?

"In the end, yes, of course. The only way forward is for the people to acquire those skills," says Jean. "But training is slow. Even when the new Technical School is up and running, it will take four of five years to get enough people well enough trained in these skills, and in the meantime, we'll still need outside people."

Could some of that expertise be supplied by people with the requisite skills from Gotera, San Miguel, or San Salvador? Even bringing in entrepreneurs from outside to run particular production projects?

"That's a tricky issue," says Anna, "because the idea of the entrepreneur has boss-versus-worker associations for people. I think there's much more of a desire in the Community to assume those roles ourselves, rather than bringing in people from outside while we just stay forever at the bottom of the ladder. We do need financial and business skills, but some people in the Community have been talking about forming small group businesses – a variation on the cooperative idea. That has much more appeal here than inviting some clown from the outside who could exploit us."

But we have noticed quite a number of Salvadorean professionals already working in the Community. There are the drivers, like Julio and Miguel, also accountants and administrators.

"Yes, that's something we need to watch very carefully. Ciudad Segundo Montes is known to have money, and there are a lot of opportunists around. You really have to be sure of people's motives before hiring them."

Juan José says, "We may not have all that much experience or knowledge, but we can see that professionals from outside aren't exactly perfect: there are lots of things they don't know. In the long run they can make things more complicated than they really are; so they're not always the best solution."

Aid for getting productive projects off the ground is one thing: CSM leaders can foresee the day when it will no longer be necessary. Aid for non-productive services like healthcare and education, which will never make money, is quite another. Here the Community finds itself caught between three alternatives, each problematic. It can continue to rely on foreign aid, but not forever, as donor agencies are increasingly emphasising; it can charge users of the services, which will be unpopular and could simply result in the services being less widely used; or it can negotiate with the Salvadorean government on ways of incorporating healthcare, education, and infrastructural services into the state system, which could endanger their grassroots and egalitarian character. The Community is negotiating with the government, says Juan José, but it is an uphill struggle.

"The National Reconstruction Plan covers restoration of roads, drainage, and so on; a few schools; strengthening local government, the return of the mayors – but nothing broader. It's also heavily influenced by the politics of the government, which are to privatise all state services gradually. Paradoxically, the state is encouraging us to be autonomous by not providing any public service or public funding. But that isn't empowering the communities at all. Besides, the government is still suspicious of the repatriated communities, so we aren't a priority for them."

CSM both benefits and suffers from its celebrity and its success at attracting aid. And it is different: people at the meeting agree that its experience is neither representative nor replicable. Jaime is convinced that, with all its difficulties, integration is crucial:

"If we don't develop the whole region, Ciudad Segundo Montes won't have a market and won't be a success. We ourselves in FASTRAS are working in a unified project with the whole region. In the end, all kinds of groups – communities, ex-combatants, the war-disabled – are part of the same project of the social movement, of building a base, reconstructing civil society. We are working on ways to support them; but we NGOs also have to find ways of negotiating and reconciling these communities with the government. A lot depends on that."

*****

We leave San Salvador next morning in Juan José's pick-up, via a succession of mean streets crowded with handcarts, grotesquely overladen buses and decrepit lorries. Above polluted gorges lined with plywood shanties, the capital's industrial area lurks behind high security fences and sculpted lawns. Beyond Soyapango we join the Panamerican highway and head eastwards back to the Community.

We take it in turns to sit in the cab or on the open back of the pick-up, bouncing around on top of sacks and boxes. The air becomes deliciously cool as the road climbs to Cojutepeque and coffee plantations beyond. The countryside is extremely lush, with flowers and creepers in a profusion of orange and purple assaulting every roof and tree. We see figures working in the fields, walking beside the road, or seated under thatched roadside shelters to sell oranges, lemons, and water-melon. Children, mostly barefoot, carry baskets of *pupusas* on their heads, to sell at the bus-stops. Women in the universal plastic flip-flops pick their way among the rubbish by the roadside, carrying water on their heads in bulbous plastic containers shaped like Greek vases.

We descend into a broad valley scarred by the lazy coils of the Lempa river, its waters brick-red against the vivid green of the maize fields. Upstream is a dam with a hydro-electric plant. Just below it, tall brick pillars stands as a forlorn memorial to the Cuscatlán bridge – one of the most spectacular victims of FMLN sabotage in the early stages of the war. We cross by a double-bailey bridge, box girders supporting wooden railway sleepers which clatter under our tyres. Only here, in the course of the entire traverse of the country, do we see soliders on guard.

We reach San Miguel about midday and pull into a turning by an imposing United Nations sign-board, to wait in the shade of some trees while Juan José goes off to a meeting of PRODERE. This organisation brings together representatives from the ministries of education, public works, and housing in the San Miguel region, with representatives of popular organisations and NGOs, including PADECOMSM and Ciudad Segundo Montes. A year ago such a meeting would have been unthinkable. Today it is a product of the peace process and the National Reconstruction Plan, and a pointer to the way *concertación*, or harmonisation, is supposed to work. Juan José says that it's still mainly a talking shop without a chair and formal agenda. The local government representatives are defensive, and often resentful of the way most decisions are taken over their heads in the capital. After an hour or so we head off back to Segundo Montes.

22
Fiesta

A big crowd, with lots of children, is gathering in front of La Guacamaya Subversiva, the San Luis cafeteria. There is to be a fiesta, to mark the completion of work to remodel the little café. First, though, there is to be a party for the children. Salsa music is blaring out from a p.a. system. and two clowns are performing on a crude stage erected in the centre of the open space. To get a better view, children have climbed onto the walls of the new SuperMontes store which is being built next to the Bank. We strain to hear, but even when we catch the words, the language and jokes are too specific and local for us to understand. The crowd rocks with laughter.

Swinging by a rope noose from a branch above is a large, brightly painted doll – a sort of caricature Barbie gone to fat. About four foot high, the creature wears a spotted clown-suit, and has garishly-painted sky-blue eyes and tufts of mustard-yellow hair. Chubby arms and legs stick out at an angle. This is a *piñata*, traditional at children's parties throughout Central America. The kids grab sticks from the undergrowth behind the Bank and begin to beat the *piñata*, while the rest of the crowd shouts encouragement. After a while the reason for the doll's obesity becomes apparent: its clothes rip at the seams and a torrent of sweets pours out into the crowd below where the children jostle to grab them.

A banner strung from the balcony of the Bank reads: 'Grand Barbecue and Dance: Saturday 5.00pm ¢12.00.' We decide to stay for the barbecue and make our way into the Guacamaya Subersiva, paying our ¢12 at the steps. Curiously there is plenty of room, and we find a table immediately, despite the crowd milling outside. It is some time before we realise that apart from visitors, international workers and non-locals like Julio the driver, none of the CSM residents has come to the barbecue: for the vast majority, who have little or no cash income, ¢12 (about 85p) is a prohibitive sum.

The tiny open terrace of the Guacamaya with its eight wooden tables is surrounded by a high wire-mesh fence, probably to keep out the animals. Several dogs are on patrol, attracted by the smell of chicken sizzling on the barbecue, and as we drink our beer a family of five ducks waddles by. But there are others excluded, too: a tall, gaunt youth with a haunted expression and deep sunk eyes is pressing up against the wire from outside, his arms extended above his head, moaning softly. This is Chico, one of several children in the Community with severe mental disability. According to his family, he was always a bit slow to learn at school. When they fled from the army in 1980 he got lost and turned up much later, quite crazy. They think the army must have found and tortured him.

Two barefoot children, aged about six or seven, stretch thin arms through the wire towards us. '*Deme pisto*' – 'Gimme some money'. This is the only time we ever see begging in the Community, here in the café by the market, right next to the tarmac road which bisects CSM at San Luis, at the raw edge of the interface between an impoverished rural community and the 'market economy'. It's scarcely surprising, but it gives us a jolt.

*****

Surrounded by guitar cases, six young people are sitting at a corner table. They look to be in their mid-teens, but in fact are older. These are the members of Conjunto Morazán, the Community's resident musical group. We notice that a couple of them are wearing T-shirts produced by the El Salvador Committee for Human Rights in London, trophies of their UK tour the previous year. Cristobal tells us how the group began:

> "The band was formed in Colomoncagua in 1981 by some old men who'd been musicians in the past. They used to rehearse on Saturdays and play the old, traditional, peasant music. As it began to take off, the old men dropped out and younger people started to join. My friend Marvin and I decided to learn the violin. We wanted to play a different kind of music, which would appeal to young people.
>
> There were some Hondurans working in the camp on public health, and trying to educate the people about latrines, hygiene, etc. So we did a song about latrines. We began to write other songs about health, or about why children should go to school. We sang about some of the campaigns, the repression, the Honduran government's attempt to force the refugee camp to relocate somewhere else, and so on. The band also took part in welcome ceremonies for visitors, religious services, marches, everything."

According to another band member, Misael, three of them fought with the FMLN:

A *piñata* for Community children   Jenny Matthews

"Two of us were very young, and couldn't really manage it, so they sent us back to the refugee camp. I was only actually fighting for three weeks, and that was after the repatriation. I was in the first group that came back from Colomoncagua on foot on 18 November 1989. The Frente [FMLN] began to call up the young ones so I went, but they sent me back almost immediately, because they said the Community couldn't do without its band."

After the repatriation, Conjunto Morazán resumed working at Ciudad Segundo Montes. In 1991 they undertook a European tour, visiting Spain, Belgium, Germany, and ten cities in Britain. Since the tour the group has rehearsed and worked professionally. Neftalí explains:

"We are paid monthly by the Community, a minimum wage. The wages are going to be reduced because every work area is going to have to generate money to sustain itself and pay its staff. We charge for concerts and we sell cassettes of our music. We're going to have to think of other ways to earn money – like selling T-shirts, posters, caps, etc.

We practise every day for eight hours. When there's a concert coming up, or some event here in the Community – like the visit of an Ambassador – they warn us in advance so that we can compose a song. After 4pm, we are free to do other things – each of us has a bit of *milpa* to cultivate.

Most weekends we're contracted to perform at fiestas or events organised by the Party [FMLN]. Next Sunday we're due to play in Gotera. We play in various places outside the Community, in La Unión, San Miguel, San Salvador – even as far away as Sonsonate.

We've played live on the radio and we've recorded two cassettes. We're working on a third at the moment, but it's difficult and expensive to hire a recording studio and pay for the technician. We have two repertoires: one is commercial music for dancing to, the other entirely our own for concerts and political events. There are groups popping up in other places now, too. The commercial ones in San Salvador just play *cumbia* (dance music), but there are some like us who play and sing about what they really feel and see."

*****

As we leave the Guacamaya cafeteria in the humid dark, the dance is starting and a queue of people is filing into the doorway of the half-completed SuperMontes store. The members of Conjunto Morazán pick up their instruments and make their way through the crowd towards the rudimentary stage. Beer is being sold near the door, the bottles submerged in water in an old oil drum in a vain attempt to cool them. Several of the young men look as though they have drunk too much already.

Later, it turns out, too many people were trying to push their way into the narrow building. The Conjunto had to abandon playing when the crowd threatened to overwhelm them and damage their instruments. Men from the Community's police force attempted to bring things under control and ordered people to go home. At some point one of the drunks, a young man called Páez – an ex-combatant from the FMLN camp near Perquín – started to threaten people with his machete.

The following day Páez was up at Quebrachos watching the traditional Sunday football games with some other ex-combatants from Perquín. The Community policemen, forewarned, went to summon him to come to the police station on the Monday morning to explain his behaviour at the dance. A confrontation developed. Páez threatened them with his machete again, the police drew their guns and Páez ended up in the clinic with two bullets in his thigh, allegedly shot from behind.

The incident will do nothing to improve the image of the Segundo Montes police force. "They do nothing, that lot," says Roberto, a

Salvadorean who works for a European aid agency. "They were at the dance, and couldn't control it, and now look. They shouldn't be armed, anyway. It's asking for trouble. They'll become just like our old oppressors."

*****

The police station is a small wooden hut overlooking the road and the market-place at San Luis. Martín, who is in charge, is smartly dressed in a khaki uniform with shoulder badges showing the emblem '*CSP: Comisión de Seguridad Pública*' [public security force]. He explains their role:

"This is a public service established under the Peace Accords. When we returned from exile in Honduras, we found we needed to set up a Public Security Force for the north of Morazán and Ciudad Segundo Montes. Our aim is to protect some of the projects which the Community has created here after a long struggle, for instance the Bank. So we went through various legal procedures to ensure that the Community could get a police force to deal with any problems of public order.

There are 19 of us. We cover Meanguera, Poza Honda, Ciudad Segundo Montes and Cerro Pando. The *Junta Directiva* chose us from people working in the various project areas. We get paid by the Community, though it's not very much.

Under the terms of the Peace Accords, the FMLN had to withdraw its fighting forces to certain designated areas. They saw that some security force must be put in place to prevent crime, muggings, and so on. The FMLN and ONUSAL agreed to support us, and the FMLN gave us some arms. ONUSAL insisted that we must have a civilian official in charge to ensure that there were no human rights violations, and that fire-arms were not used unless absolutely necessary.

We've always acted in accordance with the principles of human rights and free expression. The old authorities gave no explanation at all when they arrested someone. But we're not like that. When someone commits a crime here, we summon them to come to see us. We tell them why they've been summoned and ask them to explain what happened. They tell us what's going on, and the whole thing is conducted in a peaceful manner. So we act strictly according to the law, with no ill-treatment of suspects or anything like that.

Very often the whole thing gets cleared up here in the office. We've had various cases where there's been a fight or someone's been slashed with a machete; we've summoned both parties to appear and they've ended up on good terms without making a big thing out of it. If dialogue doesn't work, then we have to use handcuffs. We had a case here just yesterday with a young man."

"Páez?" we ask.

"That's the one. We couldn't get him to talk to us reasonably; he refused to heed the summons and threatened us with weapons. So we had to handcuff him. And we had to use the regulation weapon [a rifle] on him: not to kill him, but to arrest him. We've already reported the matter to ONUSAL and they know that he was shot. We have to report all serious incidents to the ONUSAL office. This is the first time we've used a gun in the five months we've been operating here.

"Páez was one of the ones who got drunk at the fiesta. Is there a big drink problem in the Community?"

"It's not prohibited. Anyone who wants to can drink. What we do prohibit is people making a public nuisance of themselves, using machetes in anger, etc. I'll tell you about another incident here during Holy Week. A man got very drunk and stood in the road to Perquín, preventing cars from passing. We had to go and see what was going on, and we arrested him and shut him up in a little room we've got here – a sort of prison. We can keep someone in the prison for 72 hours, but that's all. If we don't get the evidence within 72 hours, the person can go free. But if we find they're mixed up in some crime, we hand them over to ONUSAL to deal with."

"What about the courts?"

"At present everything is coordinated by ONUSAL. When ONUSAL is withdrawn we'll have to see what will happen. We could be taken over by the government, for instance, when the mayors come back to the municipalities, and form the police force here for northern Morazán."

"So will you be absorbed into the new National Civilian Police force, the PNC?"

"It depends. Some of the men may want to join, if they've got the qualifications. We don't know what level of education will be required."

"Have you had problems with outsiders coming here to commit robberies?"

"No. There have been burglaries, but we don't know if they were done by people here or by outsiders. The main problems we see are men having trouble with their wives, neighbours with quarrels, social problems. There are cases of men beating their wives (and some of wives beating their menfolk). We have to impose order on that. A man should not dominate his wife or keep women as slaves. Men and women should live as equals in the home. When children get into trouble we work with the teachers."

"Are there disputes over land?"

"Yes, we've had people coming to complain that someone has put their *milpa* on their land, and so on. Usually we resolve it by negotiation, and one side pays something to the other for the use of the land. Some families have come from outside to claim land that used to be theirs, but we tell them that under the terms of the Peace Accords, land in conflict areas is the government's responsibility: the government will have to compensate former owners. People have come from San Miguel, Usulután and San Vicente. It's important that the government resolve this soon. We haven't had any cases here of threats from former owners, not like in Usulután. Most of the owners round here didn't have much more than twenty manzanas, which is really just a smallholding. And the land here is poor."

"Do you find that people respect you?"

"Most, but not all: some don't like any kind of social order. People who like to work and get on with things support us. It's only because Ciudad Segundo Montes is an organised community that they could establish this police force and pay our wages. None of us were policemen before and we haven't had any training: we're just learning. Some of us fought in the FMLN and have had experience with firearms. We fought to change this country."

"Did you know that the Minister of Defence has publicly dubbed you 'FMLN terror forces'?"

Martín just shrugs and laughs.

23
The Clinic

Two men come over and sit at our table in the Cultural Centre to drink a Pepsi. One is Matías, a health promoter, head of the Ciudad Segundo Montes Health Committee, and member of the Community's *Junta Directiva*. The other is Rodolfo, one of two young doctors who attend the Community and the surrounding area under a programme of Médecins Sans Frontières (MSF), the French health organisation. Based in Jocoaitique, the MSF programme, which covers the whole zone, has been in place since before the Peace Accords.

We ask about the health problems of Ciudad Segundo Montes. Are people healthier than the average for the countryside in El Salvador? Does the Community's high level of organisation make a difference? Rodolfo's verdict is cautiously positive:

"The common illnesses are the same as in the rural population at large but the number of cases is lower. The main illnesses are respiratory infections and diarrhoea. There's more concerted action on the health front here. There's a health committee and a single health system. It makes for more effective action and follow-up. At the individual level, too, there's better awareness about the importance of healthy living.

Infant mortality is lower than in many parts of the country, but it's hard to be precise because there's a general lack of statistics on rural areas in El Salvador. In general I would say mortality rates here are slightly better than the national average.

There are very few infant deaths from diarrhoea and dehydration. I haven't seen a single one in the six months I've been here. I'd expect to see them in a rural community like this. Mothers are more aware, and bring the children to the surgery when they have diarrhoea.

Health promoters [unqualified healthworkers] can deal with this problem, and as their training is improving there is less need for the doctor to intervene."

All the health promoters are members of the Community, and were trained in Colomoncagua by Médecins Sans Frontières and by Honduran medical students. Since the repatriation, Matías explains, numbers have fallen slightly, but the promoter system is still working well and they are proud of some of their achievements, especially in preventing a cholera epidemic.

"There was almost a panic once people knew that cholera had reached El Salvador, and could sweep through the Community at any time. We showed a video to teach them about the disease; we had a campaign on the radio, we held general meetings about it. We put one person in each settlement to distribute chlorine house by house and to teach people about the importance of chlorinating the water. People really responded: we didn't have a single case here. There was cholera on either side of us, at Corinto and in Torola."

The water is still chlorinated: everyone collects their chlorine from a centralised depot and chlorinates their drinking water at home. An environmental health team in each settlement oversees rubbish disposal and latrine building. What about malnutrition, especially since the ending of food aid?

"In the whole of El Salvador, around 85% of the children have some level of malnutrition, at least Level 1. It's much the same, but the difference here is that there are fewer cases of severe malnutrition."

*****

We make our way down the hill from the Cultural Centre with Rodolfo and Matías, over to the long hut behind the Urban Development office which serves as the San Luis clinic. As we arrive, three health promoters stagger past, carrying a lean, scantily clad figure with a bloody bandage round his leg. It is Páez, the FMLN ex-combatant injured by the Ciudad Segundo Montes police in the shooting incident on Sunday at Quebrachos. They are carrying him to the latrines, housed in a tin-roofed hut just behind the clinic. No bedpans or commodes here, it seems.

The clinic hut is about forty feet long, divided internally into booths by wooden partitions. There is a waiting room at one end with a couple of curled and faded health education posters on the walls. There are plain wooden benches to sit on. Matías introduces us to Estanislao, in charge of the health promoters' afternoon shift. He explains that there are four teams covering the San Luis clinic, working a three-shift system. On each shift there is a midwife, a casualty nurse and two ward nurses. San Luis is now the only clinic open 24 hours. If anyone in Quebrachos, Hatos or El Barrial is taken ill at night they have to make their own way or find someone to carry them here. Emergency cases are sent to the hospital in San Francisco Gotera. Clinic appointments and prescriptions are free of charge to everyone living in the Community. "But we get people coming from outside," says Estanislao, "from Villa El Rosario and Joateca. They pay ¢2 per appointment, including medicine."

"Torola, Torola." We hear the crackle of a two-way radio in the next room, and a woman's voice repeating a call-sign. Estanislao anticipates our question:

> "The doctor isn't here all the time so the promoters on shift will log the radio message. We've got a two-way radio. When there's an emergency, we put out a call for the doctor. Sometimes we can't reach him and we have to go to look for him in Jocoaitique.
>
> At the moment they've got a radio in El Barrial. If there's an emergency, the health promoter calls up the clinic here and we have to find a doctor to go down and treat the patient or bring them back to San Luis."

We hear the squalling of a baby from across the passageway. "This one was born this morning at 8.55," says Dora, the midwife. "The mother needed an episiotomy. She'll stay here until the doctor's checked her, and then she can go home, probably later this afternoon or tomorrow. When there's only the midwife at the birth, the mother can go home when she feels ready, but if the doctor had to tend to her, she must stay here until he gives the okay." Rodolfo adds:

> "The midwives usually attend the births. They only call us in if there's a problem they can't handle. There are antenatal clinics, and all first pregnancies have to be seen by the doctor to check the size of the pelvis, and so on.
>
> Since I've been here we haven't lost a single mother. Maternal mortality is very low, something like 0.7%. If a mother has serious problems, we take her to Gotera, but there aren't many problem cases here. The midwives are very conscious about hygiene and sterile conditions, so there's not much infection."

"Here the promoters deal with most of the common illnesses," says Estanislao, "while the doctors see the more complicated cases and the chronic illnesses like epilepsy, asthma, etc. There was a lot of asthma while we were in Honduras, but with the warmer climate here there are fewer cases." Rodolfo confirms the picture:

> "The promoters get a lot of practical experience. There's a very varied pathology and they're trained to deal with all the common ailments. There are weaknesses, though, because they haven't got much formal education. We give them continuous training on the job, in the daily

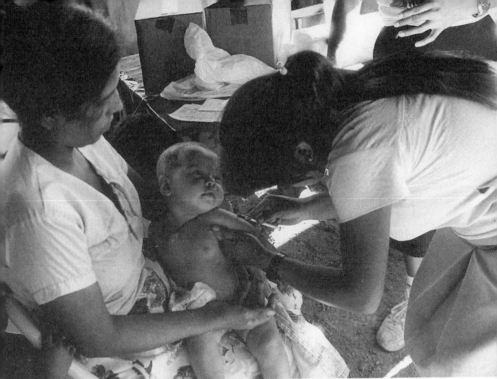

A health promoter vaccinates a baby   Jenny Matthews

surgeries, but also some formal courses, especially on respiratory disease and diarrhoea."

Recognition by the government is a major issue for the health promoters in Ciudad Segundo Montes, just as it is for the teachers. Estanislao explains:

"We don't know what will happen in two years' time, when the Médecins Sans Frontières contract runs out. There's no government clinic in the whole of northern Morazán... We're fighting to get the Ministry of Health to recognise the promoters of Ciudad Segundo Montes. The Ministry is supposed to be providing some training soon, and then it may recognise a few of us. But we want it to recognise all of us. We expect there'll be an exam, and then they'll issue some kind of diploma. If they don't recognise us, the ones who don't get the diploma will be out of work, and all the work we've put into the health of the Community over many years will have been in vain."

Rodolfo adds:

"The question is, will the Ministry recognise them only as health promoters, or will it give them the qualification they want, as nursing auxiliaries? Some of them didn't even get to sixth grade in primary school, whereas an auxiliary nurse is supposed to have ninth grade [three years of secondary school] and a nursing course after that.

The health system here is good, and could be copied elsewhere. But the Ministry of Health will want to put in its own people – its doctors, nurses, midwives, technicians..."

One alternative is to set up and register their own separate organisation, as Matías explains:

"We could convert ourselves into a non-governmental organisation – an Association of Health Promoters of Morazán – with legal status and the ability to promote health projects and get them funded. We could still have relations with the government, and wouldn't reject anything they offered. We're also considering establishing a local social security system, with contributions paid by each worker, to help finance the health system... And in the longer term, if some of the production areas start to generate big profits, they should make a contribution to pay for services such as health, education, the nurseries."

A smartly dressed woman has been sitting on a bench at the back of the room, listening to us. She is Margarita González, an academic who is doing a study for the Pan-American Health Organisation. "What you have in this community," she says, "is very close to the idea of a SILO, or local health system, which is being promoted as the model by the World Health Organisation. What's missing, though, are the links upwards, to the government."

As well as training the promoters, Rodolfo explains, the doctors give health education training to the Community's teachers, so that they can teach children the principles of hygiene and also identify any children with hearing or sight impairments.

"The problem is, we're trying to get across scientific concepts and the teachers don't have the basic knowledge to understand it.

Sometimes there are contradictions with traditional knowledge, for instance the idea of *empacho* in infants [the final stage of acute dehydration from diarrhoea]... People believe this can be cured by massaging the baby, or holding it upside down. Another traditional idea is '*el ojo*' [the evil eye]: if someone stares too much at a child, they believe it may affect the child's eyesight."

Are there any useful traditional medicines or remedies here?

"Yes, natural medicine and the use of flowers and herbs is common in this region... They certainly help to reduce reliance on drugs, especially for psychological problems. Instead of prescribing tranquillisers or a drug placebo, the patient can drink orange-leaf tea, for instance. PADECOMSM is planning a herbal garden near Perquín. They've brought in a herbalist, and he's going to install a clinic and pharmacy."

*****

As we talk we can hear splashing outside. Stripped to their petticoats, two of the women promoters have been washing their hair at the outside tap. Now one of them comes into the waiting area where we are standing, twisting thick black tresses into a gleaming plait. This is Edma, one of three promoters who are being specially trained in mental health. They have been going to San Salvador one week in four for the last five months, for training with psychologists at the Catholic university, as part of a programme funded by the Swedish government. Edma tells us about her work.

"We used to just give them pills or injections, but this didn't really deal with their problems, and was sometimes harmful. The psychologists have given us methods for dealing with mental problems and working to prevent them. The part I liked best is when they taught us about the emotions, and how emotional energy can accumulate if it isn't given any healthy release...

The war is one of the main factors, though things are better now, since the ceasefire. People complain a lot of headaches, migraine, insomnia, tiredness. These are people who want to work, but are exhausted. There's a lot of nervousness, too, especially among the mothers."

What sort of treatment do they give?

"We've set aside a room in Quebrachos. We've been taught how to complete a clinical report, and how to use a questionnaire to diagnose psychosomatic problems, depression, phobias and anything more serious. There are only the three of us doing this work and we've set aside two days a week for it. We were taught various relaxation techniques, especially for people who can't sleep. It's really lovely – I like it a lot. We've also been trained in group therapy, though we haven't had time to start it yet. We think it'll help a lot because problems get worse when people have no one to talk to about them."

*****

It is time for us to move on, as Ziortza, a Basque medical student, has promised to show us the dental clinic. We cross the tarmac road and make our way up a steep muddy path through the trees behind the Bank. A freshly-painted wooden sign points the way. Three children sit on a wooden bench, kicking their heels and looking nervous. Presumably these are the dentist's next victims. Inside, we find the Community dentists, sharing a shed with the pathology laboratory where we had talked to Elena previously. There is one table in the middle of the room, an electric fan whirring and fluorescent light overhead.

As we enter, there is a sound of copious spitting and we see an old lady in the dentist's chair leaning forward to spit blood into a tin bucket. She has just had three molars extracted. Tomás Argueta is the man in charge of the dental clinic:

"Six of us work here, but I'm the only one who has been abroad for training. At the moment we can do fillings, extractions and impressions for dentures. We can't make dentures yet, as we haven't got a furnace, but a solidarity committee in the USA has promised to send one. I've just come back from a nine-month training course there, where I learned to make dentures, bridges and crowns.

We treat people from the whole Community here in San Luis, and others come from outside as well. We used to do extractions free, but we can't do that any more. We have to charge for anaesthetics and materials, even to the people of the Community. It's ¢25 for a filling, which is the lowest price we can afford, but that compares with at least ¢50 at any dentist in the towns.

People here have a lot of problems with their teeth, and they suffer a good deal. They don't come to the dentist often because they can't afford it. We've run education campaigns about dental health for the children, the use of fluoride, but we don't have toothpaste or toothbrushes to distribute to them."

Still spitting, the gap-toothed old lady goes out ahead of us. Our own teeth somewhat on edge, we say goodbye and slither back down the path to the market place. Now we understand the little patches of dried blood we had noticed on the way up.

24
The Bank

BANCOMO, the Communal Bank of Morazán, is housed in a curious little cement block building with a balcony, set back from the road by the market-place just below the Guacamaya Subversiva cafeteria. In fact it's the only two-storey building in Ciudad Segundo Montes, and one of the very few buildings left standing by the war. The front door is open and unguarded. Inside, there are just a couple of simple desks and a few metal folding chairs to sit on.

An elderly woman from the Community has come to examine the state of her savings account. She whispers something to the woman behind the desk, who goes into the back office, finds a file and comes back to show it to the customer. She looks at it for a few moments and then hobbles away, apparently satisfied. A tall, lean *campesino* stands in the doorway, nervously turning his panama hat in his fingers, then enters, ducking his head and clicking his tongue apologetically, as people do in the countryside where there are few doors and no bells or knockers. We sit for a few moments and watch several more transactions of this kind, all conducted without any money changing hands. The atmosphere is very casual: this place seems like any other office in the Community, with none of the air-conditioned alienation of the banks in the towns, with their armed guards and brusque receptionists.

"People like to drop in and check their savings are safe, and see what interest they have earned," explains Mirna, the bank's administrator. She wears a simple skirt and blouse, but the smarter hair-style and shoes suggest someone from a town rather than a member of the Community. In fact, she tells us, she is from the city of La Unión, on the coast by the Gulf of Fonseca, at the easternmost tip of El Salvador. Like several of the trained people in the Community, she works in Ciudad Segundo Montes during the week and goes home at weekends.

"I like the Community. I started coming here during the war when very few people would come because of the danger. It's fun to take risks. And I like working where there's a real need. I was working in a university and I asked myself who needed me more – my students or this Community. I learn as well, being here. The experience of these people is very admirable."

Like many of the Community's institutions, BANCOMO started life in Colomoncagua, as Mirna's colleague, José Armando, explains:

"The idea of setting up a bank was part of the planning for the repatriation. We got some of the group in the first repatriation to act as our support in El Salvador, so we had a little team here in charge of handling currency. Back there everyone had Honduran lempiras which we needed to change into Salvadorean colones. The lorry drivers all had lempiras too, and we had to buy their lempiras from them so that they could pay for food in the cafeteria. Some needed to buy diesel or tyres for their vehicles. A lot of the visitors who supported us at the time of the repatriation had dollars and we changed these too.

We were in the midst of a war in a very isolated zone and Morazán was a major battle front. But despite all that, it was really important to set up the Bank. At first it was a mobile Bank without any kind of infrastructure. People would gather at a particular spot and the Bank would start to change their money for them. There was no vehicle.

I came in the third [repatriation] group, and it was then that we set up a base for BANCOMO here in this building. It was a bit slap-dash to begin with. We'd had a big campaign back in Honduras to get everyone to save in the communal bank and to open a savings account with the economic aid that UNHCR was going to give to each family. So when we arrived, we began to make that a reality. Each person saved half of their grant, and in that way we opened 2,000 savings accounts. It was very hard work at the time. We depended more on goodwill than skill because we didn't have a professional to teach us how to do it. But we made a start and managed to keep things under control."

Those 2,000 savings accounts still exist. They are the source both of the Bank's working capital, and its customer base within the Community. For the first year savers were not allowed to make withdrawals, but now, says Mirna, they are free to do so.

"The Bank paid interest of 10% at first. From the start, we've set interest rates at more or less the same level as the commercial banks. It's not that we're trying to compete. We're giving people a sense of confidence that this is their bank, and that their money can grow in it, and that they shouldn't need to take it out of the Community."

The Bank's capital has since been increased by a grant to fund a rotating credit scheme, and by taking in some of the international aid money directed to specific projects in the Community. CODEMO, CODECO and the other Community institutions, and all the CODECO shops now have current accounts at the Bank, and even cheque books, though these are valid only within the Community.

One of BANCOMO's main limitations, Mirna explains, is that it has no legal status. Technically, they could get fined for operating without a license.

"There are two commercial banks in Gotera, the Banco de Fomento Agropecuario and the Banco Salvadoreño...In the past they weren't interested in extending into a poor rural area like this. If we prove successful, they may change their minds. They have more resources to move around: they can set up a new branch very quickly. The Banco de Fomento does make loans in the countryside but it doesn't reach every little village. In the old days a *campesino* would never have had a bank account, not even a savings account. Only the landowners had them.

The government, too, has been setting up 'community banks' as part of its new social project. I think there's one in Gotera but it doesn't seem to work like us.

We started out focusing just on the Community, but now we see that we need to extend our work [to all of northern Morazán]. We've been considering opening a branch in Perquín, though there are limits to how much we can do. The Bank is becoming an alternative to the commercial banks, and a lot of people from outside are coming to us. It's a challenge."

BANCOMO's main importance is as a source of credit.

"We started providing credit to support Community organisations, and more recently we've extended credit to individuals in the Community who don't have work in a community project, to give them a chance to extend their activities. Sometimes two or three families get together to get a loan to buy agricultural products. This year we've had a lot more requests for loans, not just from within the Community, but also from neighbouring places: Osicala, San Simón, Cacaopera, Joateca, Perquín. We even get people coming up here from Gotera.

"People who want credit come to us and make their request. We explain the requirements. If it's a member of the Community, they must present a reference from the organisation in which they are working. If they're not in work, the reference must be filled in by the coordinator of the settlement where they live. At the same time we require them to open a savings account if they haven't already got one, for two reasons: first to make people understand that savings are necessary, though many cannot realistically save; and secondly so that their savings can serve as a guarantee for a new loan when they finish paying off the first one. In the first half of this year we made 258 loans."

What do people borrow money for?

"Mainly for agriculture, to pay for seed and fertiliser, and since the Peace Accords, to open a shop. Another common purpose is to buy cattle. That accounts for about half the loans this year. It's a way of life in the countryside, to have your pig and fatten it. Then when it's ready and the price is good you sell it. A lot of people buy and sell cattle too. No one has asked for loans to buy land. We've been asked for loans for resettlement, for instance to repair a house in Jocoaitique. We've been able to meet 90% of the requests, though we can't always respond favourably to everyone. There are limits, and we don't always lend the full amount requested.

The loans can be repaid over three years; the minimum is six months. It depends on the type of loan. There have been some bad debts, but only in some cases. It's to do with the location of our region: the war which was still raging when we got back here, and the drought which made people fall behind with their payments. We don't usually ask for any security for loans from members of the Community because we know they haven't got anything.

If a member of the Community fails to pay (there have been very few cases), we talk to their coordinator, if they are working, and then their debt is deducted from their salary payments. With those who are not working, we talk to them, explain that if they cannot pay on time, they should contact us and tell us what their problems are and we will consider extending the period of the loan."

*****

The Bank is perhaps the most ambitious of all the Community's projects, and however rudimentary in scale, it represents a considerable achieve-

The Bank   Jenny Matthews/Network

ment, much more advanced than the credit and consumer cooperatives found in some urban communities. There are limits, though, to what Ciudad Segundo Montes can achieve with its own resources (even with the help of aid agencies and the European Community), as we are reminded when we return for the night to Quebrachos.

Towering over the little café at Quebrachos is a huge building in mid-construction. It is about 25 feet high and made of the same cement block as the clothing and shoe factory. Its cavernous interior, unbroken by any internal division except a kind of gallery at one end, is hazy with dust motes floating in the late afternoon sunlight slanting through its glazed windows. Four onion-shaped ventilators crown its roof-ridge. A concrete and gravel apron, edged with channels for rainwater, allows vehicles to drive right inside. This is the Centro de Acopio, the Community's general warehouse.

We are surprised to see people working on the site when we arrive at the cafeteria for dinner at 6pm. They even have their own generator so they can work by fluorescent light. José Kalazán Márquez from CODECO (CSM's distribution organisation) explains what's going on.

"For this building we decided to use an outside contractor from Gotera because our construction workers are still inexperienced. As a result, they work more slowly which can push costs up. We needed the warehouse to go up fast, because the agency financing it had agreed the funds a year ago and was asking why it wasn't finished yet. We made it a condition of the contract that the workers had to be from CSM. The company provides the technical and administrative sides and the workers are from here."

Work only began in May and already the building is almost finished. Kalazán continues:

"When you have experienced technical people, they get the workers to calculate how long the job's going to take, and then they expect them to stick to it. I think maybe they're getting slightly higher pay, too, as an incentive, because the work is demanding."

What will be stored in the warehouse? The original idea, according to Kalazán, had been to use it to store the Community's own production of staples, but CODECO has decided to use it as a more general warehouse for 'imports' such as soft drinks, snack foods, cigarettes, toiletries, batteries, candles, and so on.

"It'll be a central distribution point from which to sell products wholesale. And not just to this Community, but also to other villages. People are coming here to buy because they get a better deal."

*****

The contrast between the Centro de Acopio and the little cafeteria beside it is stark. The cafeteria is a project too small and too under-capitalised to be viable, though for a fraction of the investment required for the warehouse, it could be transformed, and perhaps become highly profitable. The Community leadership envisage turning over such projects to the workers to run. There will be some provision, as yet unspecified, for making payments towards the value of the assets. In reality, however, unless substantial credit is given and funds for new investment provided, most of these projects are doomed.

Every night there is less to eat at the cafeteria. Last week powdered milk ran out; yesterday it was beer. The menu has dwindled to beans (mashed or whole), fried eggs, fried plantain, rice, and tortillas, the absolute basics of the rural Salvadorean diet, with only coffee or warm coke or orange squash to wash it down. The café just isn't making enough money to be able to restock anything but the basics, let alone develop a more varied or adventurous menu. Half a dozen internationals are its only regular clientele.

Part of the trouble is the café's location. Although it is well placed on the main road, it is not signposted. More important, it is outside the range of the electricity generating plant. "If we want to serve meat," says Helena, the coordinator, "we have to go and get it every day, and that means we waste time. If we leave food here from one day to the next, it goes off and we lose money."

Helena is quite clear that what the café needs is a little investment. "I've explained the need for a refrigerator [to CODECO], and for a Coleman lamp and some cooking utensils. We gave CODECO a list, and they said they'd get them for us. But we've not seen any of it yet.

We could take out a loan: I've told CODECO we could start with ¢1,000 (£70) for the moment; but we haven't got ¢1,000, only ¢500, and they haven't given us the rest. So the capital we have to invest is very small and we're struggling."

In fact, CODECO is planning to hive off the café. Kalazán readily admits that this is because it makes a loss and is subsidised by CODECO's other eating-place, the Guacamaya. He also says that the café workers need training, not just in cooking, but in running a business, costing, budgeting, and so on. They would be the first to agree. Helena says she values the experience in administration and management that working in the café gives her. It is encouraging that CODECO recognises that running a café is not just an extension of cooking for a family; the problem now is to find a trainer and organise the training.

*****

When we come out of the Quebrachos café they are still working on the building site next door at the Centro de Acopio. In the dark we stumble across the road towards our little hut. To our urbanised ears, the silence is uncanny, and yet the night is rich with gentle sound: a baby crying somewhere in one of the huts beyond the football pitch; a pig stumbling with its leg caught in its tether; frogs croaking in the thick undergrowth close to the road. Here or there the faint gleam of a candle, but for the most part people are in bed with the darkness and will be awake with the dawn soon after 4.30am. A glow of fluorescent light comes from Rudi's hut: he rigs up the light to car batteries so that he can work in the evenings.

As we cross the tarmac road in the darkness we almost trip over a line of large boulders stretching right across, about fifty yards above the speed-hump where the bus stops. In the darkness any passing vehicle is likely to hit one of the stones and crack its sump, or worse. Who would be mad enough to construct this trap? Kalazán shrugs: "Someone wanting a lift home, probably one of the ex-combatants from Perquín. It's the only way they can be sure the cars will stop."

25
New Town

The *ladrillera*, or brickworks, is a vast barn by Hatos II, open at the sides, with its corrugated iron roof supported on a flimsy framework of wood. Next to it, in a smaller shed, is the Community's pottery, with a large brick-built kiln at one end. Half a dozen women are mixing clay to make the huge earthenware griddles on which every household bakes its tortillas.

Everywhere around the brickworks are mounds of grey-coloured blocks and tiles, the latter stacked in flat spirals like giant ammonites. At one end, a team of five, mostly women, is making micro-concrete roofing tiles: applying a measured mortar mix into the frame of a bench-top vibrating unit, smoothing it with metal floats, and transferring the result to plastic moulds. The vibrator and the block-maker are the only machines in evidence. The sand and aggregate are sieved by hand and the mix is prepared with rake and shovel in large concrete vats set into the ground.

The brickworks can only make about 900 blocks per day, when the machine doesn't break down, but since construction started on the houses at Hatos and Copinolar, they need at least 1,500 a day. A new block-making machine has been ordered, with a capacity of 3,000 blocks per day, but at present it's stuck in customs. According to Inez Reyes, the coordinator, (a man, despite the name):

> "A block here costs about ¢0.95 including all costs and labour, as against ¢1.50 in commercial outlets. We should be able to sell outside the Community at some point, when we get our new machine. But first we've got to make enough for the houses of the Community. People [from outside] try to buy blocks from us, but we have to say no. We still need them all for the Community.
>
> We used to make [traditional] kiln-baked bricks, but the problem was the cost of firewood for firing the kiln. We'd buy timber from further north in the mountains, but in the winter and the rainy season, you couldn't get lorries up there a lot of the time. Most of the houses are being built with blocks. We just use bricks for things like water tanks and the washing areas."

There have been a lot of teething problems. The local sand and grit proved unsuitable, making blocks that crumbled easily. The problems with the tiles were even worse, producing irregular shapes and uneven edges as well as extreme fragility. Some of the tile-making team have just come back from a two-week course in San Salvador.

*****

Branching off the main road on the other side is a track, marked by a large CSM noticeboard acknowledging European Community support for its housing project. A young woman is grinding maize outside a very old *rancho*, the traditional peasant housing of Morazán. It is built of adobe, with some lighter partitions of bamboo. Rough wooden poles support a low roof of chaotically placed clay tiles, projecting to form a veranda a few feet wide on three sides, and half submerged by vines and creepers. The floor is of beaten earth. Much of the space is occupied by stacks of firewood. This was their home before the war, the woman explains. When they returned from Honduras they found the house abandoned and partially destroyed, and moved back in.

We continue along the track until we come out onto a small plateau, above the dispersed houses of the Hatos I settlement, with fine views across towards the Torola river and Mt Cacahuatique. This is one of the main building sites for the Community's new permanent housing. We count 19 houses in varying stages of construction, densely clustered, only about fifty feet apart, leaving little room for privacy and for the garden plots which are so important to the *campesino* household. A few have the white cement roof tiles, but it is apparent from the chinks of light shining through that these will have to be re-laid. The rest have the traditional red tiles, bought in from San Miguel.

The houses bear little resemblance to the traditional Salvadorean adobe house. Each has a front veranda, supported by massive piers at either corner, and is divided into three or four rooms. The exterior walls are almost a foot thick and reinforced with steel rods.

At the moment the only water on site is a temporary pipeline rigged up to supply the construction work. Apparently the plan is to pipe water to a single sink in the kitchen of each house. Dry latrines will be constructed behind the houses, using an alternating pit system which can provide sterile compost for use on the gardens or *milpa*. This has been tried successfully elsewhere in the zone, and works well for individual families, although it is unsuitable for communal use.

Some eighty workers are busy on the site, organised in teams by house, with the exception of a group of carpenters busily sawing and planing roof-timbers in the shade of a tree. Some women are shovelling sand and throwing it against a wire-mesh screen to sieve it. In the mid-morning heat they are working very slowly, their heads and shoulders covered by shawls to protect them from the sun.

We spot Salustino, head of Urban Development, the Community's construction organisation, talking with the carpenters. There's a lot of shaking of heads, and we guess that they are talking about the poor quality of the local timber for the windows, doors and roof-trusses. Salustino explains, as we jolt back up to San Luis in his pickup, that the timber problem threatens to add to the delays already caused by the shortage of blocks and tiles.

*****

In the office of Urban Development, Salustino has arranged a meeting for us with Porfirio, his assistant, and Lorenzo, a French technician. In the first three months of 1990 the new returnees built emergency housing in each of the new settlements with materials transported from Colomoncagua and whatever else was available – often sheets of polythene, cardboard or plywood. Although the process of settlement had been planned in detail in Honduras, the difficulties of the terrain and the need to clear trees and rampant undergrowth from every part of it made for slow and somewhat chaotic progress, and the houses were placed wherever there was free space.

Systematic measurement of lots did not start until the following year when the Community got a grant to train eight young people as surveyors. At first, the plots were too small.

"People didn't want to live so close to one another," explains Porfirio. "They needed and demanded a larger plot, with room for their gardens, and Urban Development accepted that. In the end we agreed on plots 20m wide by 30m deep, twice the size of the original."

The plan, from the outset, was to build permanent housing of brick, breeze block or adobe, with tiled roofs. In Honduras the Community had drawn up elaborate plans for the new housing 'estates', based on hexagonal clusters of houses, the brainchild of a Spanish architect who advised them at the time. Other advisers were critical of this plan, and in any case the realities of the terrain made it somewhat impractical. However, it is still being used, at least in theory.

During 1991 the emergency houses were replaced one by one by the *vivienda mínima* or 'basic house', built more solidly with a wooden frame, plank walls and corrugated iron roof, and located on a properly surveyed and measured plot. By the time of the IDEA census in early 1992, only 262 out of 1,455 dwellings in the Community were still emergency, most of them in Quebrachos.

For the permanent housing they first experimented with mud-adobe, building variants of the traditional *campesino rancho*. Although the materials were cheap, the labour-time was two to three times that required for a house built of cement blocks. Next, they built a cement-block demonstration house just opposite the Urban Development office, so that people could come and see and make suggestions and criticisms. This is the design they are using today, though it has been successively modified to economise on materials.

Selection of land for building plots has been difficult, and the problem is unlikely to get easier. Some people will have to be moved.

"We know this is a problem," says Porfirio. "We've had to move a few families already, but so far we've tried to choose places for the new building where there are very few houses. In the future, we'll build on spaces freed up by people moving into the new houses."

But won't that only free up one lot here, another there? Surely the new housing can't be built in ones and twos?

"To begin with, no. We've been building various new houses together on one site so that we can control the work better and train the work teams. Eventually, though, we could build on single sites. One of the big problems is finding level ground. That was the problem with the original [hexagonal] plan. You couldn't build like that on this kind of hilly ground, without huge costs in moving earth and rock to construct terraces."

*****

At present the Community is building 29 houses in Hatos, and 35 more at Copinolar, up the hill towards Quebrachos. They have funding for 382 houses from the European Community and for a further 72 from a French government grant. One of the difficulties with the French aid was that it was tied to the purchase of French equipment and machinery. Building work only started in March this year and they have a deadline to complete these in two years, by February 1994. Their target is to finish 145 the first year and the balance in 1993/4. The budgeted cost is ¢22,400 (£1,600) per house, including labour. The Community needs at least 1,300 houses, but it seems unlikely that more than about 600 new ones will be built, and even that will take three years.

Building the new community centre   Jenny Matthews

We ask how the new houses will be allocated.

"It was discussed at a General Assembly in April, and Social Welfare has established an Allocation Commission. The agreement was to give the first hundred new houses to Community employees who are still living in emergency housing. There are about 120 families in this group, so we will draw lots to decide between them."

One of the international workers had earlier described this Assembly meeting to us with some bitterness. Apparently there were three alternative proposals: to distribute the new houses among all employees; among just those employees who are still in emergency housing; or among single mothers. A lot of the discussion centred on the problems of women in the community and single mothers. However some of the leaders complained that the women weren't really single at all, but were 'always getting pregnant and dropping babies'. When it came to the vote the second alternative was chosen and women got very few votes.

We had also talked to the women workers building at Copinolar, who said they didn't know how allocation was going to be done. When we make this point, Porfirio comments: "They probably do know but they aren't very precise about it. These people have a lot of limitations. This is a decision which was taken with full worker participation. There was a General Assembly with one representative for every ten workers. This proposal about housing allocation was taken to the workers, to everyone. They elected their own representatives, and they knew what was going to be discussed. Maybe their reps didn't report back properly, or were confused about what had been decided."

Will the houses be free, or will people buy or rent them?

"No. The materials will be free. But the occupiers will have to repay the labour costs, about ¢5,000 in monthly quotas of about ¢20/30, over 15 years. It will be a symbolic contribution."

So will people be the legal owners of their houses?

"We're not sure, yet. Probably not until they've been paid for in full. And they probably won't be allowed to sell them to anyone outside the Community. The Community will reserve first option to buy back. The other problem is title to the plots of land. We're waiting for the government to resolve that."

The present programme won't rehouse everyone. What about the rest? Couldn't people build their own housing, with help from the Community's Urban Development organisation?

"Some may, but there's a mentality here of people expecting things to be given to them. Even with repairs, people often wait for us to come and fix things for them. We haven't been able to change that mentality."

*****

We return to the Cultural Centre with Lorenzo and Salustino. Salustino examines one of the wooden roof supports with a frown. "We'll have to repair this soon. It was built too quickly, and the structure's quite weak in places."

This complex, together with the hotel and offices below it, was the Community's first major building project. Completed in less than twelve months for the international conference in November 1990, it represented an extraordinary effort and considerable cost. Some international visitors and agency staff are openly critical, regarding the Cultural Centre as a *folie de grandeur*. Since our arrival in the Community we have seen both some of its shortcomings and strengths and some of its enormous potential. It is extensively used for the reception of visitors to the Community, especially the all-important delegations from embassies, aid agencies, churches, solidarity and human rights groups from every part of the globe (more than 950 names have been added to the visitors' book kept in the External Relations Office in the first six months of 1992).

The Centre also provides a focus for all engaged in project work in the communities of Northern Morazán. There is also a potential for tourism. The occasional car turns off the road to Perquín at San Luis and somehow find its way (there are no signs) up to the Cultural Centre. Families disembark to admire the view and buy refreshments at the cafeteria. With a bit of imagination and a little investment, this place could earn a lot of money for the Community. Somehow, though, the Centre remains separate from and largely alien to the people of Ciudad Segundo Montes itself. The leadership and those with specific responsibilities use it for small group meetings, and the teachers from the nearby Teachers' Centre are often there for overflow meetings when their own classrooms are occupied. But few others come here, except when Fr Rogelio says Mass, and for the occasional ceremony or event. No ordinary member of the Community can afford to eat in the cafeteria. The magnificent hilltop remains, as it began, the screen upon which the Community projects itself to the outside world, rather than a centre for the Community.

We ask Salustino about the architectural design work for all these buildings: is it done here in the Community?

"We're not really self-sufficient. If you think about it, designing a whole new town is a huge project."

*****

A new town. That seems to be the big unresolved question. Is this community a string of rural settlements, or is it a new town? According to FMLN leader Marisol Galindo, one of the distinguishing characteristics of Ciudad Segundo Montes is that "it didn't just happen. It was planned, and with the active participation of the people." The big challenge for the Community has been "to come out of an assisted economy into a normal economy, to produce, to compete, and at the same time to insert themselves into the zone". The FMLN hoped that the Community would help to raise the economic level of the zone, and act as a catalyst for other communities which are more *campesina*, more peasant in character, sharing with them its experience of production. So it was envisaged as a special place, less peasant in character, with more non-agricultural activity, but not necessarily as a town. Throughout our visit this same ambiguity has punctuated many of our conversations: to varying degrees everyone we speak to recognises that this is not simply an agricultural community. There are too many people, there is too little land, there are all sorts of services and facilities you would not find in a farm settlement or cooperative. The Community is managed and planned, and is building new, permanent housing in a way that is unlike any rural settlement (except possibly an Israeli kibbutz). Yet somehow it is less than a town, and balks at the small but significant changes which would transform it into one.

Lorenzo, the French construction technician, tells us that he lives across the river in the town of Osicala because there is electric light there, and he can read in the evenings. Yet when we ask him, he says that electric light is not important for the Community.

Won't the new permanent housing be a big change for people? we ask.

Salustino nods: "Hardly any of us are used to living in a place laid out with streets and fixed plots. We came here with the intention of building a town. People knew that our project, the permanent project, meant a change. Yet they were used to living dispersed in the countryside, at great distances from one another."

Now that people were settled here and started sowing their *milpas*, haven't they been drawn back towards their more traditional way of life? If so, what will happen in a few more years when the soil is exhausted and the *milpa* won't sustain them?

"People who make their *milpa* around the edges of the settlements are going to find they won't get the kind of harvest they're getting now. But they're discovering other places to work instead. And the development of the Community should provide new work centres, new employment."

Inez Reyes, the coordinator at the brickworks, had told us:

"We thought this was going to be a town, a *ciudad*, Ciudad Segundo Montes. But maybe some people don't want to live in a town, they want to live in a place which is more in the wild and work the land. As you know, in a town you can't just work any bit of land. You have to go and look for somewhere to rent. But I'm happy living here."

26
Reconciliation

On our final Sunday in Morazán, a Mass of Reconciliation is held at Osicala, the village just south of the Torola. Osicala is where the parish priest, Miguel Ventura, was arrested and tortured in November 1977. You can see at once that Osicala somehow kept itself safe during the war. It is tidy, even a little smug. The cobbled streets are lined with low tiled-roofed houses. Very little bomb damage is observable. There are even new buildings, such as the ANTEL telephone company office.

The plaza, where the Mass is to take place, is grassy and dappled with shade. Its prettiness is ruined by a bizarre concrete structure – almost certainly a military watch-tower – which looks like it was built by a three-year-old giant, with its coloured blocks of turquoise, yellow, black and red. The top storey has lookouts on all four sides. Beside this monstrosity, touchingly decorated for the day with swags of blue and white balloons, the altar has been set up on a concrete podium. It is an ordinary large kitchen table, covered with a white sheet gathered into festoons with safety pins. A scrawny kitten has gone to sleep under it. On top, pale pink roses and carnations are arranged with palm leaves and asparagus fern in tumblers and jam jars. Rogelio and Esteban, the priests, wear plain white vestments, the stoles embroidered with stylised peasant designs – an ear of corn, a house and a church, a yellow sun – over their everyday clothes. Propped against the altar are placards: 'Welcome, friends and visitors on this day of communal reconciliation'; 'To reconcile is to forgive: we want peace'. The choir – a dozen or so young people and one or two older ones, including Arminda from El Barrial – sits on the edge of the podium, waiting to begin.

Among the steadily growing crowd there is a fairground atmosphere. A Chilean song from the Allende era blares tinnily from loudspeakers strung up on the watch-tower. There are food stalls, cavorting children, people staking out places to sit in the shade.

That complete trust between northern and southern Morazán is not yet re-established is clear from the opening remarks, given by a woman from the north: "We are here to participate in a ceremony of reconciliation," she says; "we haven't come to cause any trouble, but because we are prepared to be reconciled with all Salvadoreans. So, sisters and brothers, comrades, don't worry, we don't want you to be alarmed because the police are here. We consider that we have every right and obligation to be present at a Catholic Mass."

Fr Rogelio reasserts the message of renewed unity:

"We are forming a single people here, a single family. Twelve years of war have just come to an end. In spite of all that has divided us in those years, we have always been able to see and feel the presence of God among us. God has been with us, and God continues to accompany us. And today he invites us to be reconciled, to become one single people. The Torola river is no longer a frontier. We are one Church, one people, walking together, with our beloved and suffering people, in search of a peace that will be more consolidated with the Accords."

The text for the day is woven through everything that is said. It is from the prophet Isaiah (2:4):

They shall beat their swords into ploughshares, and their spears into pruning hooks. Nation shall not lift up sword against nation, neither shall they learn war any more.

Finally, Fr Miguel Ventura arrives from San Salvador, to wild applause. He has a cold and his voice is hoarse, but declamatory, as he gives his sermon. He reminds the congregation of the debt he owes them, for it was here in Morazán that his commitment to the people was born. He expands on the ideas contained in the passage from Isaiah, asking, how is peace to be built? Are we doing enough to promote peace and to forgive our enemies? Are we really beating our swords into ploughshares? There is a sidelong reference to the differences between Catholics and evangelical Protestants in the region; the evangelicals were known to have favoured the government side in the war and were rewarded with protection and warnings from the army of approaching attacks:

"How can we raise a prayer for peace to our God if we can't open our hearts to our adversaries? We have different religions, perhaps, and how are we, who nourish ourselves with the word of God, opening our hearts to our adversaries? Sisters and brothers of Osicala, you too have suffered deeply the terrible consequences of the war. And none more than you this afternoon can raise a cry to the Almighty: 'Lord, give us peace!'"

He recounts examples of joint action already visible as signs of reconciliation:

"I would like this afternoon's message to be this: when we feel that the progress of the Peace Accords in this country is getting bogged down, and many of us wonder whether there will be a peaceful future for El Salvador – yes, sisters and brothers, there is a future for peace, because many of you have accepted that you must live with your adversaries. There are signs even now: for example, the wounded soldiers; soldiers from both the armed forces and the FMLN have begun to make joint demands, even though the war set them against each other. They are beginning to understand that the war no longer has a reason to exist. We have begun to break down the barriers that separated us."

Finally, he uses the story of Noah to stress that peace-building is everyone's responsibility:

"... before the Flood came, Noah went round preaching to the people, telling them to build an Ark, because a difficult time of trial was on its way, and those who did not build a ship would be drowned. [But] many people, instead of listening to Noah, continued going about their business. Dear sisters and brothers, I think that today Salvadoreans are again being called to build a ship, an Ark of Peace. The eyes of many are upon us, the Salvadorean people, to see whether we can build a peace that can bring hope not only to El Salvador but to the peoples of Central America and the world."

More applause; cries of 'Viva' ring out; offerings of peace – garlands, a poster depicting clasped hands – are made. A woman from Osicala makes a short speech. Some babies are baptised in the name of peace. But we learn, later, that the Mass was held in the plaza not because the fresh air is pleasant nor because the church was too small to hold the expected crowd, but because the parish priest of Osicala hadn't allowed the church to be used. Why not? Rogelio says, wryly, "He's a good man, but the thing is, he's terrified of his bishop." The bishop in question is the Bishop of San Miguel, chaplain to the army, and a die-hard conservative.

And although so many people have come, they are mostly from north of the Torola – or from the east: there are delegations from Estancia and Calavera, over by Cacaopera – but not many from the communities south of the river, except for Osicala itself, with its special connection with Miguel Ventura. Yes, there is a long way to go yet.

*****

The mountains of Morazán   Jenny Matthews

As we leave the Community at the end of our stay, we are aware that the
peace is not yet a certainty. Hard bargaining is going on between the
government and the FMLN; the demobilised of both sides are angry and
restive because they are not being given the land they were promised; the
government's imposition of VAT (for the first time) has made ordinary
people feel that they are being expected to pay for the war twice over. To
people in northern Morazán the adjudication by the World Court at The
Hague of large and productive tracts of their region to Honduras is just
another piece of evidence that those in power do not care about them –
or indeed, are still trying to get rid of them: more than one of our
acquaintances remarked that by ceding the disputed area to Honduras the
government was shrugging off 4,000 FMLN supporters (and potential
FMLN voters in 1994) at a stroke. The gulf yet to be bridged is not so
much that between poor people south of the Torola and poor people north
of it, but the age-old gulf between rich and poor, powerful and powerless.
There is very little in the National Reconstruction Plan that will help
bridge that gulf, especially if – as in the case of the land for ex- combatants
– there is no mechanism for ensuring that the Plan is fairly implemented.

Ciudad Segundo Montes is also at a watershed, poised between the novelty and danger of the return and full reinsertion into ordinary Salvadorean society. The Community is no longer a capsule; already its edges are blurring both physically and socially, as people move into and out of it, and economically, as the strictly collectivist model possible in the refugee camp is diluted by the hard imperatives of life in a dependent capitalist economy. Some people, in fact, would argue that the last thing the Community should do is to re-integrate into El Salvador's society and economy if that means creating afresh the old system where a subsistence economy existed on the margins of the national agroexport economy. One of the Community's leaders told us:

> "If we succeed in generating an alternative kind of development that will raise the standard of living for a workforce that used to provide cheap labour for the big landowners, then the landowners are going to have problems. I mean, who gives a damn about the country's economic crisis if it's the crisis of a model based on the agroexport business? And who gives a damn if the oligarchy collapses? In the end, that's what we want.

> I think that's why we're embarking on a different development process, to make a contribution to that change. Of course that has its problems too, because in these parts, under-development itself, the low self-esteem of the under-developed, has become a feature of our culture. We have to instigate a new mentality."

But the prevailing view among the leadership sees integration in terms of CSM's power to influence its surroundings. Leaders of Ciudad Segundo Montes (and aid donors) would have liked the Community to be capable of transforming social and economic relations in Morazán, if not nationally. According to Marisol Galindo, the FMLN hoped that Ciudad Segundo Montes, with its unusual skills and its attendant aid package, would raise the economic level of the zone. People in the refugee camp talked of bringing their unique experience at Colomoncagua back to El Salvador to enrich the new society. Development agencies talked of the repatriated community as a new development model. It has already become clear that many aspects of the Colomoncagua experience simply won't work back in El Salvador, and, far from being replicated in other communities, are being jettisoned at Ciudad Segundo Montes. The region's economic level is creeping upward, but probably mostly because aid agencies are now addressing the region as a whole. In the short term, as aid agencies gently disengage themselves, Ciudad Segundo Montes itself is actually becoming poorer. So far, the Community's greatest contribution to northern Morazán has been political: negotiating the restoration of the bridge, bringing human rights violations into the open, boosting other communities' confidence and readiness to make demands.

As usual, life is far richer and more diverse than it appears on paper. Ciudad Segundo Montes is valuable to the people of northern Morazán, politically important in El Salvador, and fascinating to observers and theorists, not because it is the model, or even a model, but because it is the locus for a vast array of diverse and rapidly changing initiatives, trends, reactions and spontaneous developments – some good, some bad, some useful, some unrepeatable, many adaptable, all interesting.

And what if Ciudad Segundo Montes does not survive in its present form and does not succeed in establishing itself as a semi-industrial centre for Morazán or eastern El Salvador? What if the settlements become simply a string of little rural villages again? Ciudad Segundo Montes is not only its leaders. It is also eight thousand ordinary people, who, for all their articulateness and history of organisation, have no greater ambition than to subsist with dignity. They are people for whom the Community's political and economic project may be less important than reunion with their families, resettlement on their land and making a living. These are the people whose movements and activities will weave Ciudad Segundo Montes into the fabric of the surrounding region, changing the Community's priorities and strategies by natural processes.

Yet they also have a sense of themselves as a community rather than a collection of unrelated individuals or families. Their expectations are now higher than they were, and higher than expectations in the communities around them. They now expect a community solidarity expressed in more highly socialised healthcare, education, and welfare services; they will be less tolerant of unequal structures of wealth and privilege if these threaten to take root again. Sister Anselm remembers how, before the war, the peasants of northern Morazán "would scarcely lift their heads to look you in the eye when they said hello". Their hard-won discovery of the strength imparted by community spirit and community organisation has changed that.

Ciudad Segundo Montes is a pioneering experience, and it is in the nature of pioneers to be superseded. But in whatever form it survives, Ciudad Segundo Montes will always be a little different, marked out by its singular history. In our final conversation, Juan José recapitulates the theme that runs through so much of Community discussion – the delicate balance between the ideal and the real, between adapting to necessity and safeguarding the best of exile's lessons:

"It would be nice to think that the Community will go on being like Colomoncagua, all homogeneous, all headed in the same direction; but I think it's getting harder and harder to see that happening. If we accept that our guiding principles are participatory democracy and self-management, then we're contradicting ourselves. For participatory democracy should imply opening up space for different ways of thinking to arise. And self-management itself means an impulse towards decentralisation.

Increasingly, our most pressing problem is how to support ourselves, and this period is so critical that practically all our energies are being absorbed in working out how to stay afloat. This is also sapping our idealism and causing a great spiritual void which we are very aware of. People say, 'Well then, where on earth are we going?' I think that right now it's very hard to say whether we're capitalists, or socialists, or communists – it hardly matters what, as long as we survive!

This is one of the things that makes us different: we want to survive, but in a way that ensures the majority benefits. We are apparently the most privileged community in this zone. It's true that practically all the aid to Morazán is concentrated here. So we must start looking at our priorities again, our capacities, our resources to see how the small benefits we have here can also be extended in other directions. The difficult thing is that we arrived here living purely on aid, and if aid were to disappear tomorrow, how would we support ourselves?

But then, our critics have been predicting that the Community will disappear ever since we came back. And we're still here!"

27
Epilogue

Two years have passed since we visited Ciudad Segundo Montes. It has been a testing time for El Salvador. Implementation of the Peace Accords has been patchy and partial, and feelings of betrayal and disappointment are general. Despite a fairly respectable result for the FMLN on its first exposure to the ballot box, ARENA won a convincing victory at the March 1994 elections, which were held simultaneously for President, the entire National Assembly, local mayors and municipal councils.

From the outset, the former adversaries have had differing conceptions of reconstruction. For the FMLN and the popular movement, the job of the National Reconstruction Plan (PNR) should have been to lay the foundations for economic development in the former conflict zones through the 'new popular economy' – the survival strategies devised by poor people, including cooperatives and the various resettlements such as Ciudad Segundo Montes. The government, however, saw reconstruction principally in terms of rebuilding major infrastructure, had only a secondary interest in alleviating poverty, and none at all in the sort of economic models that would empower poor people. In practice the PNR has prioritised ex-combatants, and principally the officers of either side, in its programmes. The repatriated and repopulated communities have received little or nothing, even though they contain many ex-combatants.

Land distribution under the Accords is generally admitted to have been disastrously mismanaged. By March 1994 only about 20 per cent of the land earmarked for redistribution under the Peace Accords had been transferred to 11,270 of a proposed 47,500 beneficiaries. Never clearly defined, the land transfer process has become more and more confused: former owners cannot be found, or have died intestate; records have been lost or destroyed; the courts and the government bureaucracy are incapable of handling the volume of petitions and disputes; and the political will to deal with the morass is absent.

On human rights, progress has been even worse. On 15 March 1993 the Truth Commission published irrefutable evidence of high-level armed and security forces involvement in all the worst human rights violations of the war. On the massacre at El Mozote it concluded that all the people in the village on 10/11 December 1981 had been 'executed deliberately and systematically' by members of the Atlacatl Battalion under the command of Col. Domingo Monterrosa in the course of 'Operation Rescue'. The Salvadorean authorities had 'failed to order any investigation and continually denied that any massacre had occurred', and the president of the Supreme Court had played 'a partisan and political role in the judicial proceedings'. These conclusions were backed up by forensic evidence gathered from El Mozote itself, where the skeletal remains of 143 people, 131 of them children under twelve, were exhumed in late 1992. However, the government refused to accept the Commission's report and on 22 March, just a week after its publication, issued a general amnesty pardoning everyone named in it.

Reform of the police force has also been uneven, while crime and banditry, and possibly deliberate destabilisation by former military or paramilitary men, have risen alarmingly. Worst of all is the apparent resurgence of rightwing terror. Between the signing of the Peace Accords and the March 1994 elections, thirty leading FMLN members were reported killed in ways bearing the hallmarks of the old death squads.

*****

No longer welded together by military imperatives, the FMLN began to fragment in 1993, particularly over economic policy. The ERP, one of the five organisations comprising the FMLN and the dominant force in Morazán and the eastern part of the country, moved towards a social democratic political stance and accommodation with the prevailing neoliberal model. When it began replacing cooperatives in Usulután with small businesses, its leaders were accused of opportunism and neglect of social processes, and a breakaway group called the Democratic Tendency was formed. Although we could not observe these differences at first hand in Ciudad Segundo Montes, the conflicts that developed there appear to mirror closely what was happening on a national scale. Despite the rifts, which no doubt cost votes, the FMLN emerged from the elections as El Salvador's second largest political force. Predictably, it dominates the former conflict zones. In Morazán, the FMLN won the municipalities of Meanguera, Jocoaitique, Perquín, Arambala, and Villa El Rosario. The new municipal council of Meanguera consists entirely of CSM people.

*****

Ciudad Segundo Montes has not been immune from any of the problems that beset post-Peace-Accords El Salvador. There have been conflicts over land and difficulties integrating the 586 ex-combatants who settled in the Community. The CSM leadership insisted that they had occupied the land in 1989 by agreement with the government and that the national Land Bank must take responsibility for negotiating land sales. With no sign of this happening, former owners' willingness to sell to the Community wilted. A number formed an Association of Former Landowners, allegedly affiliated to ARENA, which issued threats against CSM residents. Some FMLN ex-combatants and their families also demanded their original lands back, producing further tension.

Meanwhile, the building programme continued, with completion of the Technical School, a new health centre at San Luis, new schools, factories and bakeries, and a physical rehabilitation centre for the war-disabled. Together with the new housing, the appearance is of a much more built-up area than when we were there. The telephone line was installed, and electric power extended to a few individual households in San Luis. About 400 new houses had been built by mid-1994, but quite a few still stand empty because families cannot afford them, and BANCOMO, which is starved of capital, has stopped providing mort-gages. Those who can buy tend to be Community employees. Others retort, bitterly, "Well, if you don't have work, how on earth are you going to pay for a house?"

The key social provision of health care and education has continued, but many items which were previously free now have to be paid for. The schools are flourishing, but the battle over certification of the popular educators continues, with the universities offering crash courses to provide as many of them as possible with the formal requirements.

*****

FMLN leaders originally saw Ciudad Segundo Montes as the 'economic motor' of northern Morazán. Its skilled workforce, combined with the aid funds it could attract, were to lay the foundation for recapitalising the zone. However, the comparative prosperity of CSM did not obligingly 'trickle down' or ripple outward. On the contrary, deep fissures opened up within the Community itself, as access to wealth and decision-making became increasingly concentrated in the hands of the *Junta Directiva* and the Community employees. The base of political participation narrowed until only a few hundred employees were eligible to vote. Communal

Services, the only remaining community forum not formed out of employment sectors, withered away, and with it the key services for the 'vulnerable sectors' such as widows and the elderly.

All this depressed morale. Even favoured Community employees became dissatisfied with top-down management and near-nominal political participation. Rumours of nepotism and corruption spread. Workers felt the profits they generated were not returning to the Community but disappearing centrally, and unaccountably. The Community had never really developed structures for accountability and democratic controls on its leaders. The latter, preoccupied with ensuring the Community's economic survival (and their own), had sidelined its political development, although, to give them their due, the topic was often discussed.

Apparently, three strands of thought emerged in the *Junta Directiva's* economic discussions, all revolving around different concepts of ownership of the Community's assets – land, housing, workshops, equipment and materials. A few, fearing the loss of the old solidarity, clung to the centralised 'Colomoncagua model'; others favoured transforming this into a form of communal ownership; a third group, the majority, proposed devolving the management of the workshops and other Community enterprises to cooperatives, although details of ownership and payment for assets remained hazy. This process was beginning at the time of our visit. Several workplaces had formed cooperatives and begun independently seeking work when, in mid-1993, some members of the *Junta Directiva*, possibly fearing the loss of their own power, suddenly turned fiercely against the decentralisers, acccusing them of betraying the ideals of community solidarity forged in Colomoncagua.

Disagreement erupted into open conflict in July 1993, when five international workers were sacked over their support for a group of carpenters who had allegedly used Community equipment and worktime to carry out a private contract. From the dispute emerged an organisation aspiring to represent the interests of all the workers of the zone, the Association of Workers of Morazán (ATM). It was strongly supported by the workers at the electricity plant, who had formed their own cooperative of users as well as workers, the Morazán Electrical Energy Cooperative (CEEM). Ex-combatants, resentful at the over-concentration of power with the *Junta Directiva* and their own lack of a voice in the Community, were active in both these organisations. Simmering hostility between the *Junta Directiva* and the CEEM came to a head in December, when the latter cut off electricity supplies to the Community for failing to pay its bill. Whereupon a group of people, including several *Junta Directiva* members, broke into the plant and assaulted and ejected the cooperative members who were guarding it.

*****

Recent visitors to the Community report that conflict has subsided, leaving a more peaceful confrontation of differing viewpoints. The *Junta Directiva* has admitted to 'errors' and declared its commitment to greater internal democracy, although it still answers only to the 'organised' sectors – the Community employees and organisations such as the women's group. The result of the municipal council elections should help. Now that the FMLN and Ciudad Segundo Montes people control Meanguera municipality, they can administer legal local government structures integrated into the national state, relieving Ciudad Segundo Montes of the burden of operating an entire parallel government.

There is talk of creating a 'voluntary association' to own and run the Community's large economic projects, consisting of project workers and other Community bodies such as the war-disabled and women's organisations. The workshops are increasingly more autonomous: the clothing and shoe factories, for instance, are flourishing, having won contracts to make uniforms for the new national police force.

Despite its difficulties, CSM has not fragmented irreparably, nor reverted to a string of peasant villages on a subsistence economy, but remains a viable semi-industrial community. The population has fallen, but only gradually, as some groups have sought better land in Usulután, and others have returned to family lands. Economists working with CSM regard this as no bad thing, given the incapacity of the land and the potential labour market to sustain a large population. Different settlements are taking on individual characteristics, most notably Quebrachos, which lies within the municipality of Jocoaitique, to which it increasingly looks.

While the dwindling of social services such as the nurseries has increased the workload of single mothers, it is noticeable that the workplaces where women are in the majority are the most successful. A recent European Union evaluation identified the conservatism of peasant culture, particularly among men, as a brake on the Community's development as a semi-industrial centre. It is principally the men who keep alive a pair of myths which we heard articulated many times. One is an idealised reconstruction of pre-war Morazán as a world where every-one was content, subsisting on their own land; the other harks back to

Colomoncagua as a golden age of unity, solidarity, and limitless aid. But the old Morazán is gone and Colomoncagua is a windswept ruin. Slowly the myths and the ideals that bore these people home in the midst of war are giving way to the realism they need to survive the peace.

September 1994

Appendix A
Glossary of Spanish words

asamblea	assembly
asentamiento	settlement, village
barrio	neighbourhood
calle negra	the 'black road', the tarmac road from San Francisco Gotera through CSM to Perquín
cantón	ward, small sub-division of a municipality
campesino	peasant
capturado	captured, kidnapped, arrested
caserío	hamlet, small cluster of rural homes, valley
carpa	tent, hut
catequista	catechist, catholic church lay activist
centro de acopio	central distribution warehouse
chele	blond or fair-skinned person
ciudad	city, town
colón	the Salvadorean unit of currency, approx = 7p (1992)
colonia	neighbourhood
comedor	dining-room, cafeteria or café
compa, compañero/a	FMLN fighter, comrade, companion
comunal	communal, community
concertación	harmonisation
concentración	assembly point (for guerrilla fighters)
cuajada	a kind of curd cheese
cumbia	dance music
cusuco	armadillo
Desarrollo Urbano	Urban Development – CSM's building works department
desmovilizado	demobilised, e.g. FMLN or Army fighter demobbed for return to civilian life
educador	teacher
empacho	(lit. = congestion) the last phase of dehydration by diarrhoea
encargado/a	supervisor
estructura	structure, organisation, one of the formal areas of work providing employment within the Community
estructurado/a	having a defined role/paid job in the Community
fiesta	party, festival
Frente, el Frente	the 'Front', i.e. the FMLN
frijol, frijoles	bean(s)
granero	cylindrical grain storage bin
guacamaya	parrot

guaro	strong cane spirit
hectarea	unit of land area, hectare 1 ha = $10,000 m^2$ = 2.47 acres
hotelito	'little hotel', guest-house
junta directiva	the executive or leadership committee
ladrillera	brick works
lisiado de guerra	war-wounded, disabled veteran
machete	broad-bladed knife-cum-scythe universally carried by men in the Salvadorean countryside
maestro	teacher, skilled worker, expert
maguey	*Agave americana*, sisal plant
maicillo	sorghum
matacaballos	'horse-killer', a venomous spider like a tarantula
manzana	measure of land area (= 10,000 $varas^2$ = 0.71 hectares = 1.75 acres)
meta	target, norm
milpa	small plot of land used for growing subsistence crops
mozo	hired farm-hand
municipio	municipality, borough
ojo	eye, the evil eye
organismo	administrative department of the Community
parcela	garden plot
pila	outdoor sink for washing
piñata	doll filled with sweets
pisto	money, cash (slang)
pita	sisal fibres
pupusa	pasty of maize dough filled with mincemeat or cheese
pupusería	shop or stall selling *pupusas*
rancho	traditional peasant house
refrigerio	snack-meal
retén	army checkpoint or road-block
taller(es)	workshop(s)
tarea	measure of land area 1 tarea= 900 $varas^2$ = 0.09 manzanas = 0.06 hectares = 0.16 acres)
tierra	land
tortilla	flat, round pancake of maize bread, like a small pitta
viva!	Long live...!
vivienda	house, dwelling
zona, La Zona	the Zone, Morazán north of the Torola River, the zone controlled during the war by the FMLN
zopilote	vulture

Appendix B
Glossary of Acronyms and Organisations

ADIM   *Asociación para el Desarrollo Integral de la Mujer*
       Association for Women's Integral Development

ANTEL   *Asociación Nacional de Telecomunicaciones de El Salvador*
       El Salvador's Telephone Company

ARENA   *Agrupación Renovadora Nacionalistta*
       Far-right party of government

BANCOMO   *Banco Comunal de Morazán*
       The Community's bank

ATM   *Asociación de Trabajadores de Morazán*
       Association of Workers of Morazán

CARITAS   International Catholic aid agency

CDHM   *Comisión de Derechos Humanos de Morazán*
       Morazán Human Rights Commission, based at CSM

CEBES   *Comunidades Eclesiales de Base de El Salvador*
       Christian Base Communities of El Salvador

CEEM   *Cooperativa de Energía Electrica de Morazán*
       Morazán Electrical Energy Cooperative

CIAZO   *Campaña Integra de Alfabetización de la Zona Oriente*
       Eastern Zone Integrated Literacy Campaign

CIREFCA   *Comité Internacional para Refugiados y Desplazados en Centro America*
       International committee of agencies working with the refugees and displaced people of Central America

CODECO   *Comité de Desarrollo de la Comercialización*
       Marketing Development Committee, CSM's wholesale distribution organisation

CODEMO   *Comité de Desarrollo [y Emergencia] para Morazán*
       Development [and Emergency] Committee for Morazán

COPAZ   Commission for Peace, a government-FMLN commission established by the Peace Accords

CSM   Ciudad Segundo Montes

CSP   *Comisión de Seguridad Pública*
       Temporary civilian police force established under the Peace Accords in Ciudad Segundo Montes and other FMLN-controlled areas

DM4   *Destacamento Militar No 4*
       The Fourth Division of the army, based in San Francisco Gotera, the capital of Morazán.

END	*Ejercito Nacional Democrático*
	National Democratic Army, the FMLN's guerrilla army
ERP	*Ejercito Revolucionario del Pueblo*
	People's Revolutionary Army, the largest of the guerrilla groups making up the FMLN, dominant in Morazán
FASTRAS	*Fundación para la Autogestión y Solidaridad de los Trabajadores Salvadoreños*
	Salvadorean Workers' Foundation for Self-Management and Solidarity
FMLN	*Frente Farabundo Martí para la Liberación Nacional*
	Farabundo Martí National Liberation Front
FUSADES	Salvadorean businessman's organization
IDEA	*Iniciativa para el Desarrollo Alternativo*
	Initiative for Alternative Development, a San Salvador based research organisation which carried out the census of CSM
MCM	*Movimiento Comunal de Mujeres de Morazán*
	Women's Communal Movement of Morazán
MSF	*Médecins Sans Frontières*
	French health NGO
NGO	Non-governmental organisation
ONUSAL	United Nations Peacekeeping Force for El Salvador
PADECOMSM	*Patronato para el Desarrollo de las Comunidades de Morazán y San Miguel*
	Council for the Development of the Communities of Morazán and San Miguel
PNC	*Policía Nacional Civil*
	The new civilian police force due to be established under the Peace Accords and replacing the old and discredited National Police which was under military control
PNR	*Plan Nacional de Reconstrucción*
	National Reconstruction Plan
PRODERE	*Programa para Desplazados, Repatriados y Refugiados en Centroamérica*
	Programme for Displaced People, Repatriates and Refugees in Central America
RV	*Radio Venceremos*
SILO	A local unitary organisation for primary health care, as promoted by the World Health Organisation
UES	The national University of El Salvador (with campuses in San Salvador, San Miguel and elsewhere)
UNDP	United Nations Development Programme
UNHCR	United Nations High Commissioner for Refugees

Appendix C
Chronology

July 1969	Four-day 'Soccer' War between El Salvador and Honduras
1972	First guerrilla groups formed
20.02.77	Fraudulent election of General Humberto Romero
28.02.77	Massacre at Plaza de la Libertad, San Salvador, when demonstrators protest at election fraud
	Founding of Ligas Populares 28 de febrero, popular organisation linked to ERP
03.11.77	Fr Miguel Ventura, parish priest of Osicala, captured and tortured at DM4, San Francisco Gotera. Left the country soon after release
19.07.79	In Nicaragua, Sandinistas march in triumph into Managua, while dictator Somoza flees
15.10.79	General Romero ousted by 'young officers' coup', bringing initial hopes of return to democracy and human rights
1979	First refugees cross into Honduras
03.01.80	Guillermo Ungo, Social Democratic leader, resigns from the first post-coup government, marking the defeat of progressive elements in the new government
22.01.80	67 killed and 250 wounded by National Guard at demonstration in San Salvador's main square
24.03.80	Archbishop Oscar Arnulfo Romero assassinated while saying mass, by a death squad organised by Major Roberto D'Aubuisson
18.04.80	Formation of the Democratic Revolutionary Front (FDR)
10.10.80	Army launches first scorched-earth sweep in Morazán
12.10.80	1,000 people flee across border to Colomoncagua
13.10.80	Massacre at La Guacamaya
Nov 1980	Formation of the FMLN guerrilla co-ordination
27.11.80	Murder of five members of FDR Executive Committee by army and police in San Salvador
12.11.80	1,000 people flee to Colomoncagua
21.11.80	Napoleón Duarte inaugurated as President
02.12.80	Rape and murder of four US missionaries and nuns by Salvadorean National Guard
Jan 1981	FMLN announce 'final offensive'
Dec 1981	Army launch Hammer and Anvil operation in Morazán
11.12.81	Massacre at El Mozote
12.10.82	FMLN guerrillas occupy Perquín, Torola and San Fernando

26.10.82	FMLN take Joateca, the last army redoubt north of the Torola
17.01.83	FMLN blow up the Torola bridge, south of Meanguera, cutting off the 'zone'
23.02.83	Army abandons Perquín, leaving FMLN in control of whole zone
31.12.83	Honduran government and US embassy launch campaign to relocate refugees from Colomoncagua
23.10.84	FMLN forces blow up helicopter, killing army commander Domingo Monterrosa, held reponsible for El Mozote massacre
14.05.85	Virtual state of siege imposed at Colomoncagua
29.08.85	Three killed and 54 wounded in Honduran attack on camps
13.09.86	Salvadorean airforce bombs Callejon Hill close to Colomoncagua camp
06.08.87	Esquipulas II Central American Peace plan signed
10.10.87	First group repatriation — 500 Salvadorean refugees return home from Mesa Grande camp in Honduras
April 1988	Military Operation 'Perquín I'. More refugees cross to Colomoncagua
13.04.88	PADECOMSM founded in ceremony at the UCA, with 55 communities from Morazan
23.05.88	Honduran soldiers kill refugee, Santos Vigil, in Colomoncagua camp
23.05.89	Colomoncagua refugees tell CIREFCA of their wish to repatriate
12.10.89	Fr Segundo Montes gives seminar in San Francisco Gotera on repatriation
31.10.89	Death squad bombs headquarters of FENASTRAS trade union in San Salvador
11.11.89	FMLN offensive begins with attacks on San Salvador and major cities
16.11.89	Six Jesuit priests, including Fr Segundo Montes, and two domestic staff, assassinated at UCA
18.11.89	712 refugees repatriate on foot in first group from Colomoncagua
23.12.89	Sr Antonia crosses the Torola River on stepping stones to make the first contact with CSM
14.01.90	Main mass of Colomoncagua refugees commence repatriation. Camp is dismantled
23.01.90	Repatriation of group to repopulate San Luis
Feb 1990	Sandinistas defeated in Nicaraguan elections
27.02.90	Completion of repatriation. Colomoncagua camp closed
25.03.90	Inauguration of Ciudad Segundo Montes

23.06.90	New bridge over Torola river opened
17.11.90	Ciudad Segundo Montes hold international conference to mark their first anniversary. Inauguration of Cultural Centre
18.11.90	FMLN assault on San Francisco Gotera. Ciudad Segundo Montes conference plans disrupted
12.01.91	Efigénio Márquez Vigil from CSM captured in San Francisco Gotera by DM4
10.02.91	National Vaccination Day. Army prevents medical teams from going to northern Morazán
17.08.91	Army attack on CSM leaves 34 wounded
11.12.91	10th Anniversary of El Mozote massacre. Army puts up 14 checkpoints between San Miguel and the river. No one gets through
Dec 1991	Food aid discontinued at CSM
16.01.92	Peace Accords signed in Mexico City
01.02.92	Ceasefire and end to violent confrontation
22.03.92	Attack on CSM lorry in San Miguel and theft of ¢60,220

Index

89, 132, 141, 169, 179, 199
Protestants 111, 190

Quebrachos 12, 22, 23-30, 31, 32, 33,
37, 44, 46, 50, 62, 63, 65, 90, 97,
99, 100, 119, 127, 130, 134, 151,
162, 167, 171, 178, 180, 184, 185,
200

radio 10, 16, 21, 35, 81, 90, 105,
128, 162, 167, 168
Radio Segundo Montes 11, 105
Radio Venceremos 10, 35, 120
rancho 182, 184
reconciliation 7, 146, 189
refuge 26, 27, 41, 56, 79, 102, 103,
116, 117, 138, 145, 146, 153
refugees 5, 6, 9, 12, 15, 16, 17, 18,
27, 34, 38, 47, 48, 52, 53, 54, 55,
56, 67, 68, 69, 75, 81, 83, 90,
98, 103, 108, 112-118, 123, 125,
131, 145, 154, 160, 161, 193
refugee camps, see Colomoncagua and
Mesa Grande
repatriation 9, 15, 17, 19, 48, 52,
53, 54, 56, 57, 67, 68, 83, 91, 97,
98, 104, 107, 108, 118, 125, 131,
136, 154, 156, 161, 166, 174
repopulation 51, 79, 133
rivers 5, 6, 7, 13, 15, 19, 21, 24, 35,
47, 58, 60, 64, 76, 80, 86, 103, 112,
122, 128, 156, 159, 174, 188, 190,
191
roads 5, 6, 7, 9, 11, 13, 14, 17, 18,
21, 23, 24, 30, 31, 32, 34, 37, 38,
46, 47, 50, 51, 52, 53, 54, 56, 58,
62, 73, 76, 80, 81, 109, 111, 112,
114, 118, 119, 120, 127, 150, 152,
158, 160, 163, 164, 172, 173, 179,
180, 182, 187
Romero, Archbishop Oscar Arnulfo 2,
35, 36, 52, 120, 121, 145

Salvadorean government 5, 33, 53, 56,
116, 157
San Francisco Gotera 6, 9, 14, 20, 23,
36, 57, 58, 69, 79, 109, 114, 150,

151, 167
San Luis 9, 10, 11, 12, 17, 20, 21,
22, 23, 39, 46, 48, 62, 68, 77, 79,
86, 90, 106, 107, 110, 111, 131,
134, 136, 137, 143, 151, 159, 160,
163, 167, 168, 172, 183, 187, 198
San Miguel 20, 28, 36, 43, 47, 60,
69, 83, 109, 121, 152, 156, 158,
162, 165, 182, 191
San Salvador 1, 35, 37, 38, 45, 46, 47,
69, 71, 82, 83, 87, 90, 93, 100, 111,
120, 123, 150-158, 162, 171, 182,
190
Sapo river 35
savings 173, 174, 175, 176
schools 9, 11, 14, 17, 18, 21, 24, 27,
28, 31, 33, 49, 50, 51, 53, 77,
105-111, 115, 117, 123, 124, 128,
133, 157, 160, 170, 198
security forces 34, 153, 163, 196
self-sufficiency 15, 16, 26, 28, 87,
132, 136, 138, 187
shops, see also SuperMontes 9, 10, 20,
21, 24, 31, 33, 36, 47, 61, 74, 80,
83, 110, 113, 120, 123, 125, 130,
133, 134, 135, 152, 158, 175, 176
SILO 170
single mothers 80, 100-103, 133, 136,
138, 168, 186, 200
sisal, see also maguey 7, 62, 65, 83,
100, 119, 133, 140
skills 21, 27, 28, 75, 97, 116, 117,
125, 130, 131, 140, 156, 193
social services 15, 25, 74, 75, 86,
136, 138, 200
Social Communication 11, 141
Social Welfare 77, 141, 185
socialism 29
soldiers, see also army 7, 11, 23, 36,
41, 43, 44, 54, 57, 58, 60, 77,
100, 113, 114, 115, 118, 120, 148,
150, 152, 153, 191
solidarity 12, 17, 27, 48, 70, 90, 116,
126, 137, 146, 154, 172, 187, 194,
199, 201
sorghum 62, 63, 64, 65, 67, 113
Spanish aid 183
subsistence 24, 62, 64, 65, 98, 119,

Are you looking for more infomation on Latin America?

At the Latin America Bureau, you can discover:

Books: theme books, country guides, women's studies, Latin American authors in translation

Recent titles include - On theLine: Life on the US-Mexican Border, The Latin American City, Rebel Radio: the Story of El Salvador's Radio Venceremos

Magazines: for consultation and by subscription

Day Schools and Evening Classes: for the non-specialist

A library in London; for digging deeper

Contact us for further details:

Latin America Bureau, 1 Amwell Street, London EC1R 1UL
Tel: 0171 278 2829
Fax: 0171 278 0165
E-Mail: lab@gn.apc.org